Table Decoration

Frontispiece. A "pineapple" of daffodils. To make it, tie a cluster of daffodil leaves to a light bamboo stick, and with green florist's thread, encircle it with daffodils until the size and shape of a pineapple is attained. Cut the stems off about two inches below the last circle of daffodils and bind firmly. It will stand erect in a shallow dish without any need of support, making a spectacular centerpiece in the spirit of the 18th century. *(Arrangement by the author; photograph by Francis Lambert)*

Table Decoration

YESTERDAY, TODAY, & TOMORROW

by Georgiana Reynolds Smith

CHARLES E. TUTTLE COMPANY
Rutland, Vermont & Tokyo, Japan

Representatives
For Continental Europe:
BOXERBOOKS, INC., *Zurich*
For the British Isles:
PRENTICE-HALL INTERNATIONAL, INC., *London*
For Australasia:
M. G. HURTIG, LTD., *Edmonton*

Published by the Charles E. Tuttle Company, Inc.
of Rutland, Vermont & Tokyo, Japan
with editorial offices at
Suido 1-chome, 2-6, Bunkyo-ku, Tokyo

Copyright in Japan, 1968
by Charles E. Tuttle Co., Inc.

Library of Congress Catalog Card No. 68-21113

First printing, 1968

Book design & typography: Florence Sakade
Layout of plates: Shigeo Katakura
PRINTED IN JAPAN

To MARGARET FAIRBANKS MARCUS
without whose help and encouragement
this book would still be largely a disorganized collection
of notes in a card catalogue

Table of Contents

List of Illustrations

II

Acknowledgments

To me the most reassuring thing in the course of my pursuit of this elusive subject has been the willingness of busy and scholarly people to help and guide me in the unfamiliar complexities of independent research. That so many important people have taken time and trouble in my behalf has greatly encouraged me to feel that my small discoveries in this very minor branch of the decorative arts might have genuine interest and value. To the following I would like to express particular appreciation:

Dr. Rudolph Berliner, who in the early 1950's as curator of the department of decorative arts at the Museum of Art of the Rhode Island School of Design gave me the first breakthrough in my search for useful sources of information. As a result of a fortuitous interview with this patient and courteous gentleman I acquired introductions to two of the happiest hunting grounds: the Houghton Library of Harvard College and the Library of the Boston Athenaeum.

Philip Hofer, curator of the department of printing and graphic arts at Houghton Library, who spread before me many examples from his remarkable collection of fete books, a form of literature I had not known existed.

Gertrude Townsend, a personal friend and curator emeritus of the department of textiles at the Museum of Fine Arts, Boston, who in the course of her own research often came across something that had bearing on my subject and took the trouble to send me explicit directions for locating it. She also led me

15

to many other fruitful sources including early dictionaries and books of reference, which I would have been quite unlikely to discover by myself.

KATHRYN C. BUHLER, another friend and former assistant curator of the department of decorative arts (Museum of Fine Arts, Boston) as well as an international authority on American silver, who gave me the benefit of her criticism and advice.

Of the many patient librarians who provided cheerful and willing service to an inexperienced researcher a few must be mentioned personally: CAROLYN E. JAKEMAN of Houghton Library, MARGARET HACKETT and DAVID M. K. McKIBBIN of the Boston Athenaeum, MARJORIE CHILDS of the Boston Museum of Fine Arts, and MURIEL C. CROSSMAN of the Massachusetts Horticultural Society. I would also like to thank EDWARD DI ROMA, executive assistant of the New York Public Library who made prompt and scholarly replies to my letters when I found that some of my necessarily hurried research there was incomplete.

Friends outside the museums and libraries have also given me valuable assistance: JEAN GORELY, well-known authority on Wedgwood and secretary of the Wedgwood Club of Boston; NINA FLETCHER LITTLE, another well-known collector and writer on antiques.

At this point I must say that the writing of this book has been for me a formidable problem. Only one person, my good friend MARGARET FAIRBANKS MARCUS (with whom I had had a happy association in selecting and making flower arrangements for her book, *Period Flower Arrangement* in 1952) could have pulled me out of the Slough of Despond in which I found myself. She gave me confidence in the value of my research and offered constructive criticism, chapter by chapter, with keen editorial discernment. As a member of the staff of the Cleveland Museum of Art, her background of art history was helpful and some of her personal research on early uses of flowers was made available to me.

GEORGIANA REYNOLDS SMITH

Dedham, Massachusetts

Introduction

"A DINNER table in the 18th-century manner" said the schedule. It sounded like such a charming project, that first assignment, so long ago, to make a "period" table decoration at the flower show.

I was confident that it would not be too difficult—simply a matter of finding the right container, an original 18th-century piece if possible, and selecting flowers of equally elegant and gleaming texture, delicate colors, and fine form. They would be arranged either with the graceful, spirited charm of the rococo or with the closely set, pointed precision of the classic revival, depending upon the container selected. I was sufficiently familiar with the flower prints and other delightful flower designs of both 18th-century styles, I thought, to have a fairly clear idea of what was wanted.

There was only one problem. I did not remember ever actually seeing any such flower arrangement depicted on an 18th-century dinner table! This seemed very strange. To have flowers on the table is such a natural, logical, perfectly familiar idea that we have come to think of it as a long-standing tradition and have assumed that flowers must always have been a customary and almost inevitable accompaniment to a meal in any sophisticated and luxurious society. That this detail could have been omitted in the flower-loving 18th century seemed inconceivable! Yet when I began to search for specific examples, not only in that century but in preceding periods, there were apparently no such examples to be found.

Flower-show time came around and my arrangement had to be made, authentic or not. It evidently satisfied the judges for it won a prize, but it did not satisfy me. The lack of documentary evidence of flowers on the table in past centuries was a mystery that I felt compelled to solve.

Hours spent in the library produced, at first, not a crumb of evidence to support my hopes. Insofar as recorded history was concerned, table decoration seemed to be a forgotten subject. Food and table manners—or the lack of the latter—were discussed at length by many writers on manners and customs, but any embellishment of the table purely to please the eye, with or without flowers, was apparently either unnoticed or did not exist.

There were numerous references to "centerpieces" in the books on old china, but these were chiefly concerned with their importance as ceramics and not their use. Books on silver and glass also held the same point of view, always

FIGURE 1: Medieval king at table. From a German woodcut, 1491.

addressed to the collector of antiques. In museum galleries and print rooms I examined innumerable banquet scenes from the Middle Ages through the 18th century in woodcuts, illuminated manuscripts, tapestries, paintings, and engravings, but all seemed to point to the conclusion that no floral decorations for the table were ever used. That inevitable pattern of scattered cups, bowls, and ewers appeared on every table, with never a sign of a flower to be discovered. It was even flatly asserted by one art historian that table decorations were unknown and that flowers were never used on the dining table until the 19th century. This statement aroused my indignation as well as my curiosity and I went on, convinced that some evidence would eventually be found to refute this preposterous verdict.

I did not know where to look next, but luckily I suddenly stumbled upon something which led me to a completely new and infinitely more fruitful trail. This was the single mention by a 17th-century writer of having flowers on the dining table "so that the eye, as well as the palate, might be delighted."[1]

Here at last was justification for that persistent conviction of mine. It was not wishful thinking, after all! People did use flowers on the table long before the 19th century, and if one writer had mentioned them, perhaps others had even described how they were arranged. Literature, and not art, was to hold the key to the mystery!

I started excitedly along this new path which proved to have many fascinating byways. It was for me a rather unfamiliar territory, but fortunately I had friends who had traveled this way for research in other fields. They led me to letters, memoirs, and diaries written by observing people of other centuries who moved in the world of fashion and were entertained at many of the courts of Europe. Most amazing were the chronicles of eyewitnesses at medieval feasts who wrote detailed accounts of elaborate state banquets and court festivities. I learned that at the 1468 wedding of Charles the Bold, Duke of Burgundy, the banquet table was decorated with "thirty plateaux in the manner of gardens" and at another 15th-century feast the center of the table was "like a green meadow surrounded with flowering branches to which violets and other sweet smelling flowers had been attached." This table boasted tower-like cages for singing birds, their feet and beaks splendidly gilded.

In the 17th century, Mme. de Sévigné commented frequently upon the sumptuous decorations at the fetes of Louis XIV at Versailles, railing at the precariously high pyramids of fruit and voicing her astonishment at the lavish use of flowers—"a thousand crowns worth of daffodils alone!"

In the 18th century, Horace Walpole, with his meticulous eye for detail, never failed to note a new fashion in "table furniture," whether "temples and pyramids of strawberries and cherries" or "harlequins, gondoliers, Turks, Chinese, and shepherdesses of Saxon china." Other indefatigable and observing writers supplied me with many more such details.

I was fascinated, but still puzzled. Why were there no pictures of these extraordinary decorations? Perhaps in the early pictures the scattered dishes, goblets, bowls, and ewers were merely symbols (Plate 3), an easy way for an artist to say "This is a banquet table," just as he might put a crown on a man's head saying "This is the king" even though in reality the king wore his crown only on occasions of great ceremony and not every time he entertained a small company at dinner. Did the absence of table decorations mean there were none or simply that the artists considered them unimportant? I noticed that often no food was shown in the dishes and surely no one would take this to mean that nothing was offered at a royal banquet!

For some time the question remained unanswered, but I continued to read whatever firsthand accounts I could find. Many more descriptions were found, but there were still no pictures.

At length I discovered a source of information which supplied them, for the painstaking men who designed great feasts had no intention of allowing their efforts to be unappreciated. Many a head steward, proud of his skill and obviously educated beyond the opportunities of the average servant, took time out to write voluminous accounts of how he "arranged the sideboard for the Saxon Ambassador," how to construct a pyramid of fruit, how to set the "Grand Table," or how to "dress out the Dessert." Many of these books were handsomely bound volumes, souvenirs of royal weddings or other important occasions, lavishly illustrated with engravings by well-known artists. There existed also an astonishing variety of early cookbooks and books on household management which often included amusing diagrams and pictures as well as details of table etiquette.

It was this humble form of "literature" which at last provided an explanation—an absurdly simple one after all the mystery I had made of it—of why decorations seldom appeared in pictures of banquet scenes. It became clear that all decorations were reserved for the grand climax of the meal which was the dessert. After the serious business of eating was over and the great chargers of game birds, meat pies, and other succulent dishes were carried away, the table was cleared and it was time for a lighter note, with gaiety and diversion to accompany more delicate fare. Borne in with music and ceremony by a procession of lackeys were those fantastic high pyramids of fruit or flowers, spectacular sugar ornaments, and curious "machines" to delight and entertain the company. Often the dessert itself was the essential decoration. The beauty of fine fruits and the proud achievements of the confectioners, enhanced by the elegant containers that were devised to set them off, were enough to make sure that "the eye, as well as the palate, might be delighted."

Little by little tiny fragments of evidence were gleaned in these out-of-the-way sources, zealously collected and finally pieced together until their pattern became clear. Often some early notion of table decoration which at first had seemed either childish or grotesque could be traced in various interpretations through the centuries and recognized as the origin of some familiar custom in use today. Before long it was evident that practically every custom and convention of the table today has its roots in the past.

In my journey of exploration and in the solution of this little mystery, I have had a fascinating personal adventure often filled with the glow of triumphant discovery in spite of long intervals of frustration and bewilderment. I have "met" some delightful people and have attended in their company all sorts of gala entertainments, seeing with their eyes the elaborate decorations designed not only by court florists and head stewards but also by some of the foremost artists of the time. It was the rule rather than the exception to exact this kind of service from available artists, however high their standing. In the 17th century, Le Blond is said to have made decorations including flower arrangements for Louis XIV's fetes at Versailles. In Russia, according to Christopher Marsden in *Palmyra of the North,* designs for wine fountains and "ornamental trees" were made by Rastrelli, the Empress Elizabeth's chief architect, for the wedding of Catherine and the Grand Duke Peter. Marsden also says that Pineau, a French artist of considerable importance at the Russian court (1725–26), was called upon to make festive garlands of fruit and flowers upon occasion.[2] These men were doubtless assisted by lesser artists or apprentices in carrying out their ideas and sometimes one of these was assigned to the official post of "Table Decker."

Many more such bits of evidence of the importance of table adornment must be waiting to be discovered in obscure volumes on the dusty library shelves—hopeless, of course, to find them all. My progress has been slow and the territory a vast one. I have been beset by limitations of time and language, but I have at least blazed a trail which others may want to follow.

And why should anyone care to follow? Well, the mountain climber says that he must climb the mountain simply "because it is *there*." Anyone with a taste for research has much the same point of view. The distant, the mysterious, the seemingly unattainable has an irresistible appeal, but for the practical minded there is a use for this information also. It is a veritable gold mine of ideas which may be adapted to our present needs.

It is true that few of us today have either the means or the desire to entertain with medieval splendor, with 17th-century magnificence (Plate 4), or with the elegance and sparkle of the 18th century. The very words "splendor" and "magnificence" are out of place, out of date, and out of the question in our streamlined, often servantless existence. Our ways of doing things are dictated by our way of living which calls for flexibility instead of rigid etiquette, for adaptation instead of imitation, for individuality instead of a slavish following of "the Mode." Nevertheless we will find in the extraordinary and often charming table decorations of other days a surprising number of suggestions for making today's table individual and attractive.

Formality today is a relative term, but to a certain degree it is still possible and sometimes desired. As for elegance, that is not necessarily a matter of either formality or expense. It is often found in the attention to little details, in an appreciation of form and color, in a cultivated sense of the fitness of things, in a thoughtful selection of table appointments and flowers, whether for a simple or an important occasion.

Our casual way of living has its compensations, and we have learned, through do-it-yourself necessity, that informality has possibilities of great charm. The only danger is that it may make us lax and lazy so we overlook the little amenities that can contribute a pleasant background to social intercourse. Perhaps a certain degree of formality could be restored even to everyday living. Breakfast and lunch on the kitchen table may be the easiest, and necessary way. But is there not, even in the family circle, a place for candles on the table at dinner in a setting less conducive to the toleration of "kitchen manners" and carelessness of personal appearance?

It has already been observed that leaders of fashion have set a trend toward a "new elegance," possibly because they want to be different from the average person who has copied their ways of making informality attractive. Knowing that few hostesses can afford to wear a Dior gown and preside over a smoothly served full-course dinner for a dozen seated guests, they are quite safe from imitation this time. But it is a good trend, all the same, and it may filter down, eventually influencing many in modest circumstances. Candles on the table have been called "yesterday's necessity, today's magic," surely a form of magic available to all. The flower show has taught us how to make the most of a few flowers or even a little foliage or fruit. If one craves elegance within a limited budget, one can set a handsome fresh pineapple (Plate 1) or a fine artichoke upright on a compote or on a teakwood stand to make a centerpiece rivaling an 18th-century faïence ornament in the shape of a fruit or vegetable.

It is the seeing eye, the zestful approach, the imaginative ability to adapt ideas of past or present to one's own needs that can make the art of table decoration a fascinating "personal adventure."

FIGURE 2: Pineapple plant with variegated foliage in a jardiniere. Extremely fashionable in the late 19th century, unusual ornamental plants of this type were often used on the dining table. (*From* Beautiful Leaved Plants *by Lowe and Howard, London, 1891; courtesy, Massachusetts Horticultural Society)*

 ONE

Changing Fashions in Table Decoration

THE TRUE story of table decoration is far more fascinating than the one we have imagined it to be. The facts are surprising, not only because they are so different from what we might have expected but also because, in spite of the many changes, there are so many similarities to the problem as we know it today.

For one thing, even in this changing world the hostess herself has not changed so very much after all. Her basic aims and desires are what they have always been: to please her guests, to be up-to-date, to take pride in her table appointments, and to furnish some sort of an agreeable surprise to make a party memorable.

The shape of every new centerpiece also finds its counterpart in the past, though specific ones appear and disappear as temporary fashions come and go. Many familiar ways of adorning the table spring from remote beginnings. The garlands we use on formal tables have for centuries had the significance of a gracious tribute and the import of especial ceremony. The delightful scenes which we may assemble on the Christmas table with miniature figures, houses, animals, and trees had their origin in the Middle Ages when such settings were made of pastry or marzipan. Decorative foliage has been used to enhance fruit since the Romans used it in the 1st century B.C. And ornaments of porcelain, glass, silver, or other materials have often been found sufficiently beautiful in themselves to make a delightful centerpiece without benefit of fruit or flowers.

Perhaps the most significant difference between the table settings of the past and our own is that until the end of the 19th century they were designed and executed almost entirely by men, which is a surprise because we are apt to think of table decoration as strictly a feminine pursuit. But from the neat stylized arrangements of lotus blossoms or exotic foliage placed by Egyptian slaves amid stands of fruit and other produce, to the pincushion-like bowls of gypsophila and sweet peas which were the sacred prerogative of the Victorian head gardener, men have traditionally taken charge whenever the adornment of the table for a party was being planned.

One may venture to wonder, of course, if there was not very often, even in the far distant past, somewhere in the background a woman to give an eye to the decorations and other general arrangements and set the seal of her approval and the hallmark of her personality upon the scene. Even Nefertiti herself (Plate 5), that beautiful and sophisticated queen of ancient Egypt, may have supervised the placing of bowls of lotus or chosen the intricately fashioned necklaces of flowers to be worn by banquet guests (Plate 6). Looking at her serene profile, with that well-bred air of having everything under control, we may take her to be, if not the prototype, at least the symbol of the discriminating hostess we would all like to resemble

Today's hostess, alas, does not have Nefertiti's minions to do her bidding. In all probability she not only has to arrange the flowers, but cook and serve the dinner as well. But if she has the faintest glimmer of the eternal spirit of hospitality, she will make some small gesture in compliment to a guest that will lift even an impromptu party just a little above the level of daily routine. It is a dull hostess indeed who can find no means and no desire to do as much. In fact, the brightest ones make the everyday table so attractive that little is needed to give it "company" rating.

Every clever hostess today is constantly looking for "ideas" for table decoration, and she is as likely to find them in some early fashion "old enough to be new" as in the latest modern solution to this often recurring problem.

The key to all customs of the table in any period may be found in that one word "fashion." Whatever is "in fashion" is done, and if it is not in fashion, even the most charming idea is cast into oblivion—until the day when some forward-looking leader in taste rediscovers it as something "new." And it *is* new, when seen with the eyes of another century.

"Indeed, what is Fashion?" asked Horace Walpole. "Is it not a persuasion that nothing was ever right till the present moment, and that the present moment will immediately be as wrong as all its predecessors?" This 18th-century gentleman, fourth Earl of Orford, gardenist,[1] man of letters, and initiator of "Gothick" taste at his Strawberry Hill estate, belonged to the world of fashion and knew whereof he spoke. His question, and his quickly provided answer, was not so much cynical as a simple statement of truth, as valid today as it was in the 18th century.

To unravel the tangled skein of circumstances causing fashions to change and to find out what it is that makes a fashion "right" for one moment and not for the next is an intriguing study, in the course of which we discover that satiety is by no means the only reason for change. Many other factors are involved, social, economic, emotional, even political, and these furnish clues to changes in regard to table decoration as in other arts. Fashions that seem to happen "overnight" are only the climax of a gradual evolution that has been going on for a long time because of changing conditions in the world at large. When conditions are "right," the fashion, long developing, has a broad appeal and suddenly "catches on."

The spirit of a period is the distillation of the influences and accidents that have occurred within it. Despite wars and violence, cruelty and injustice, creative imaginations seem always to have been active, craftsmen's hands busy, and designers excited over new materials and receptive to fresh ideas from faraway lands.

There was the beginning of contact with the exotic East, when Crusaders and adventurers brought back impressions of undreamed-of splendors and Oriental magnificence, striking envy and the desire for competition in the minds of medieval kings and princes of the Western world. There were rare shells from newly discovered beaches, a wealth of fantastic beauty so valued that Renaissance and 17th-century goldsmiths mounted them in gold or silver to be used as cups or ewers on the high table or for display on the buffet (Plates 7 and 132). There was mysterious and beautiful porcelain from the Orient which, it was cunningly rumored by the Chinese to discourage imitation, "had to lie underground for a hundred years" before its exquisite translucency could be achieved. There was the magic of Venetian glass, offering a new and exciting way of enhancing the fruits for the dessert (Plate 124).

From one country to another men traveled, slowly because of the difficulty and danger of travel but remarkably fast when one considers how much energy and courage it must have taken to travel at all. And as men traveled, creative imaginations, ready to ignite, were fired. This is the way fashions were made in the past and are still being made today. Every new use of a material and every new interpretation of an older fashion differs from the original because it inevitably bears the stamp of a different culture and of its own century. Horace Walpole's "Gothick" differed from medieval Gothic in more than spelling. It was unmistakably 18th century, a charming surface decoration with a mannered precision quite unlike the spontaneous outpouring of faith so evident in the art of the Middle Ages. Thus, while being derived from an older fashion, Walpole's "Gothick" was nonetheless expressive of his own time which was cynical, gay, and sophisticated. Walpole "collected" Gothic—fragments of stained glass or carvings of wood or stone often found lying about in the ruins of some ancient abbey or stored in the barns or attics of a friend's country house. He used these fragments in his own way, much as an antique collector today might use an 18th-century wine cooler for flowers or an old weathervane as an ornament on the wall above the fireplace.

Walpole's unique way of using Gothic design set a new fashion, and "Gothick" influence (or "Gothique," to use the still more mannered term for this revival) began to appear in art, architecture, and even literature. In due course, as with every fashion, the idea found its way into table decoration, reflecting there also the new craving for romantic and naturalistic forms, welcomed as an antidote to the restrictions and solemnity of measured classicism.

Thus fashion, so logically induced by the prevailing spirit of the time, provides the answer to the facts about table decoration in the past. Pictures are misleading for artists wanted only to give an impression of banquet scenes and were not concerned with fashions in table dressing. For their purpose it was enough to show a few scattered functional utensils and to indicate the wealth and importance of the host by including one or two splendid gold or silver goblets or some other expensive table appointment. But early cookbooks leave no doubt that there was nothing sparse about the way tables in the Middle Ages and during the Renaissance were actually set (Fig. 3).

Hospitality was lavish and extravagant. At one feast given by the Count de Foix, a great feudal lord of the 15th century, there were twelve tables with seven courses at each table and, for each course, each table was served upon one hundred and forty silver platters.[2] These platters were piled high with rabbits, capons, venison, and small birds of passage known as ortolans arranged in pyramid form. The dishes entirely covered the surface of the table, leaving no room for decoration except for the strewn herbs and flowers used to garnish the meat and for the fantastic way in which some of the dishes were ornamented.

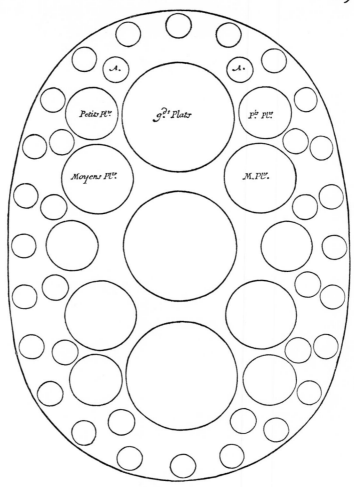

FIGURE 3: Diagram of a 17th-century table setting for twenty-four, from *La Maison Reglée* by Audiger, 1692. Specific food is designated for the three large center dishes, the four medium-sized ones, the six smaller ones, and the twelve surrounding plates. Guests now have plates instead of trenchers. *(Courtesy, Boston Athenaeum)*

Roast peacocks and other birds were served with their plumage on (Plates 8 and 122), or game pies were garnished with head, wing, and tail feathers of the bird inside. Even the simplest pie might have its pastry covering intricately cut out in an elaborate pattern of lattice work.

That there is so little evidence of the use of flowers on the table in any century is at first the most difficult thing to understand. This is especially puzzling about the 18th century, a period when flowers and flower forms were used extravagantly in all sorts of decoration, when gardening was a fashionable pursuit both for ladies and gentlemen, and when Wedgwood and other potters were busily making innumerable vases and even flower holders of ingenious design. It is astonishing to read in an 18th-century book on household management that fresh flowers were only to be used on the table when not enough artificial flowers happened to be available! But when one reflects that this was an age of artificiality and that there was a particular pleasure in "a secret artifice" or "an agreeable surprise," one begins to understand that a porcelain rose, or even one of silk or sugar so exquisitely made that it might easily deceive one into thinking it real, might indeed have been more valued than a rose which anyone might pick in the simplest garden. Rarity, extravagance, cleverness, and make-believe were "right" for the particular moment and therefore were much preferred. After all, as Sacheverell Sitwell reminds us, in *Great Flower Books,* "persons who are blasé, and have lost their sense of wonder, are not in the right mood to apprehend beauty in a humble flower."

This worldly wise point of view was manifested in many other respects, very gradually bringing about refinements in ways of living which were more appealing to the sophisticated than the old hearty customs of the Middle Ages. In those days everyone ate amid the noise and confusion of the great hall with high-ranking members of the household and important guests at the "high table" on a dais at one end of the room while lesser guests and all retainers sat at long tables on the lower level. Meat was cut up with a knife, eaten with the fingers, and the bones tossed to the numerous dogs who often fought under the table for a succulent morsel. Service was equally crude with platters and other serving dishes taking up the center of the table so that there was no room for decorations, other than garnishing, until the meal was finished, and the table was cleared for dessert.

But in the 17th century there was a significant change which made dining a more pleasant and elegant affair, for in splendid houses, whether newly built or remodeled in the new fashion, there was a trend for a separate dining room where the family and favored guests could enjoy a welcome sense of privacy. Service for this smaller, more exclusive group could also be more sophisticated. Forks came into fashion and the carving could be done outside the dining room with the dishes passed, one at a time to each guest thereby allowing space in the center of the table for elaborate decorations of one sort or another which could remain in place throughout the meal. This was, in fact, the beginning of "the centerpiece" very much as we know it today.

Curiously enough this refinement in the matter of service appears to have originated in Russia, for, later on when the system became more generally adopted it was always referred to as "the Russian Service." But whether or not from Russia it seems to have been introduced into Europe via Italy. English travelers in Rome in 1688 reported their surprise at seeing huge sugar ornaments and vases of flowers already on the table when they entered the dining room at a banquet given there by Lord Castlemaine, the English Ambassador.[3]

In France this fashion was in full swing by the 18th century, and the type of centerpiece composed of the dessert with its accompanying sweetmeats, porcelain figures, and flowers on a mirror plateau was known as a "dormant," meaning that it remained "sleeping" upon the table until the time came for the dessert. Often it was not disturbed even then, for the real dessert was brought in from outside, leaving the most beautiful creations of the confectioner untouched. As one foreign visitor exclaimed, according to that indefatigable traveler, Lady Morgan, "the French Dessert speaks to the soul, as well as to the eyes."

Immediate acceptance of this new way of doing things was not found in every court, however. In Austria, in 1740, we see a table covered with food, and service is in the old manner with a server and a carver stationed opposite to one another at every four places.[4] Two stands of fruit do show an attempt to use at least part of the dessert as decoration in the new fashion (Plate 9).

In England, though the idea may have been followed in court circles it was evidently not widely adopted even in the late 18th century, for James Woodforde, a Norfolk country parson, was astonished at the novelty of "A most beautiful Artificial Garden in the Center of the Table" when invited to dine with the Bishop of Norwich. What seems to have impressed him most, as he remarks in his diary of September 4, 1783, is that "it remained at Dinner and afterwards." Still later, in 1820, when Maria Edgeworth, the much feted Irish writer, was entertained at dinner in Paris, she expressed surprise that "on entering the dining room we saw only a round table covered with fruit and sweetmeats, as if we had come in at the dessert. . . ."[5]

In England and America, though the new idea had been introduced by the ultra-fashionable, it was generally the custom well into the 19th century to clear the table entirely after the main course whereupon the dessert was set forth on the bare table with great precision in the matter of placing the "corner dishes," the wine decanters, and the smaller plates and *tazze* of fruit and sweetmeats. The ceremony of removing the cloth, as described by an English lady in the 1850's, was a difficult and exacting task requiring the dextrous services of three or four footmen on each side of the table while two more servants held aloft the heavy epergne of fruit. The butler stood at the end of the table watching the process critically until exactly the right moment for him to perform his duty of gathering up the neatly folded cloth.[6] Since all the serving dishes had been on the table up to this point, the cloth could have become badly stained and its removal imperative.

The idea of having the dishes passed one at a time to each guest, which we consider traditional, was not adopted in the average English household with pretensions to fashion until even later. The "Russian Service," which eliminated the need for carving and serving at table and for the elaborate business of "drawing the cloth" was acclaimed by Mrs. Beeton in her book of household management (1868) as a wonderful new fashion, elegant and practical. She warned, however, that "unless the servants are very active and intelligent many blunders are likely to be made."

To understand fluctuations of taste in any era, one has only to study books of etiquette, including those of our own day, remembering that such books only reflect the taste of the period in art and in the art of living after a major trend is observable. But by that time leaders of fashion, those who started the trend, are looking for something new. Etiquette books of even a generation ago are amusing, if not entirely ridiculous. Even taste itself may have changed.

Victorian writers on table decoration speak very earnestly about "good taste and refinement, fitness and propriety of admixture" and then proceed to describe what seem to us tasteless little horrors known as "March" stands (Fig. 4), a quite ordinary version of the epergne, dripping with moss, ferns, forget-me-nots, and "love-lies-bleeding." Or they may advocate an extra leaf made for the dining table of common pine boards, with a hole cut in the middle so that a potted plant could emerge brightly as centerpiece, as recommended by Annie Hassard in *Floral Decorations for Dwelling Houses* (1876). (For today's use of a potted plant on the table, see Plate 10.) It is said that two tablecloths must be used, "carefully pinned round." Of course the cloths *must* be white, "with a green felt cloth beneath," as all 19th-century authorities insist, otherwise no dinner table would be "correct."

Clearly books of etiquette are for followers of fashion. Leaders of fashion are leaders because they do not resist change. On the contrary, they often wel-

FIGURE 4: "March" stands with fruit and flowers, 1861. This group created a sensation at a flower show in London. It was exhibited by the Misses March and won first prize. *(From* Floral World and Garden Guide, *1862; courtesy, Massachusetts Horticultural Society)*

come it, not just for the sake of change but for the challenge of meeting new conditions with imagination and taste.

The greatest challenge today, perhaps, is the acute service problem. What a revolution that has made in today's fashions! At first there were flurries of dismay. The tradition of elegance and formality inherited from the Victorians was not easily broken, and, indeed, *was* not broken until the problem became almost a universal one. A solution was eventually found by those imaginative and independent people who changed their way of living to suit new conditions.

It is no accident that we now find ourselves occasionally eating casual but attractive meals on trays (Plate 2). If buffet suppers must supplant formal affairs, comfort and a relaxed hostess need not be sacrificed for lack of service. Guests do not mind filling their own plates at the buffet if they can carry them to a beautifully set table instead of balancing them precariously on their laps.

The popularity of the chafing dish and the casserole, the acceptance of place mats at dinner, and a thousand new ways of doing things that your great-aunt would say were simply "not done" have all come to our rescue. Modern mechanical wizardry, also, has provided us with the means of coping with what had seemed insurmountable difficulties.

The challenge of informality is that it can be, in some ways, more attractive than formality. Stuffiness has "gone out." Nothing is too simple to have style, as witness our handsome kitchen equipment with beauty as well as utility in cook-and-serve dishes and everyday table appointments. Most hostesses will agree that it is better to face this change to casual living than to fight it to the point of frustration and despair.

Perhaps the best thing about today's way of life is the growing importance of individuality. It is no longer necessary to conform or to be "correct." There is no social stigma in "doing our own work." We can be ourselves and do what presents itself as attractively and with as little appearance of effort as possible, setting our own standards and living up to them as best we can. I say "appearance" of effort because of course some effort is necessary unless we wish to reduce our parties to lack-luster affairs or give up entertaining at home altogether and just take everyone to the club, a line of least resistance which can be helpful in a pinch but can become a depressing habit. Some guests are worth taking a little trouble for. They would feel uncomfortable, of course, if the effort were too obviously apparent, but it is possible to gear a party to one's own capabilities so that no one will be unduly aware of any wheels going around.

The best example of perfect table service is given in the old French fairy story of *Beauty and the Beast,* when Beauty's father in the Enchanted Palace sat down at a table spread with a magnificent feast and was "served by invisible hands" (Plate 11). Isn't this the way a meal *should* be served, smoothly and easily without unnecessary bustle or overambitious folderol to interrupt the good story or the good talk? The table looks charming; the food appears, also attractive to look upon; you eat it and it tastes delicious. You did not notice how it got there or how it was taken away. Fairy story, indeed!

And yet it is not impossible for a smart hostess in the 20th century to make her own magic with the aid of mechanical appliances and personal ingenuity. She will welcome today's challenge to provide an attractive setting for such a meal, choosing with discrimination whatever strikes her fancy, suits her budget, and expresses her personality, remembering that today, fortunately, "the fashion" is to be *herself*.

PLATE 1: A contemporary table. Here is style and charm in a sophisticated yet simple setting. An everyday centerpiece easy to achieve is provided by a fresh pineapple carefully selected for its handsome top and placed upright on an attractive compote, flanked by modern white pottery candlesticks. *(Setting, courtesy of Mrs. Hardwick Moseley; photograph by Francis Lambert)*

PLATE 2: Luncheon on trays in the garden. This sweetmeat dish, made of real shells to look like a porcelain shell dish, holds tuberous-rooted begonia buds and white grapes. An attractive service for dessert is achieved with 19th-century Canton china and painted tin trays. *(Arrangement by the author; photograph by Zitso Studio)*

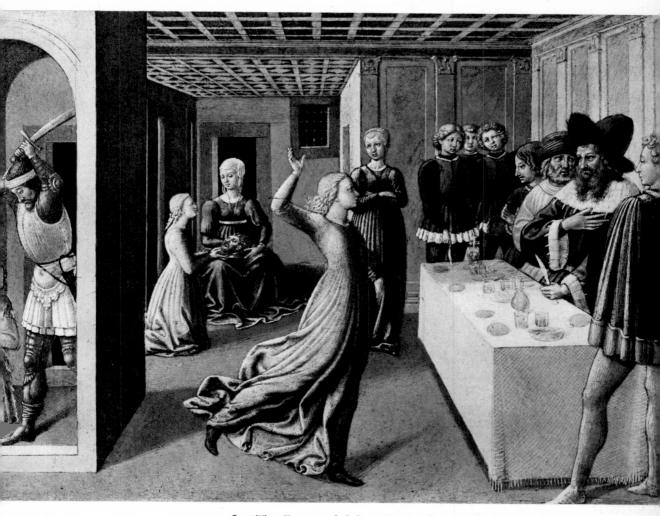

PLATE 3: "The Dance of Salome," (detail). In this painting the artist, Benozzo Gozzoli (1420–97), depicts the new Venetian glass on the table as a symbol of wealth and splendor. Notice that there is no food on the table except for the individual round loaves of bread and a little wine in the decanters. *(National Gallery of Art, Washington, D.C.; Samuel H. Kress Collection)*

38

PLATE 5: Queen Nefertiti; from a plaster cast of the painted limestone original in Berlin, *c.* 1370 B.C. *(Metropolitan Museum of Art, New York; Rogers Fund, 1925)*

PLATE 6: Egyptian queen welcoming a guest. Behind her are jars and dishes on a well-stocked pantry shelf. *(Drawing by Norman de G. Davies;* Tomb of Nefer-Hotep; Egyptian Expedition, *Vol. IX; Metropolitan Museum of Art, New York, 1933)*

PLATE 7: Nautilus beaker. Mounted on silver stand and embellished with mother of pearl cut scroll work and engravings, this piece takes after Callot of Italian comedy figures. *(Museum of Fine Arts, Boston)*

PLATE 8: The Vow of the Peacock; a special ceremony in the Middle Ages. The peacock's skin and feet were first carefully removed, keeping the feathers intact. The bird was then roasted on a spit, with a damp cloth protecting his crest. When he was done, the feet and feathers were replaced, the crest freshened up a bit, and he was ready to be served by a lady—never a servant—who was selected either for her beauty or her importance. Each gentleman in turn was then expected to make some vow of bravery or love "in the name of the peacock." *(From* Histoire d'Alexandre, *Manuscript illumination, mid-15th century; courtesy, Detuit Collection, Bibliothéque Nationale, Paris)*

PLATE 9: Servers and carvers. Servants are stationed at intervals on both sides of this 18th-century Austrian table. Herbs and flowers garnish the meat, and there are two ornamental stands for fruit. *(Engraving from a 1740 fete book honoring Maria Theresa; courtesy, Harvard College Library)*

PLATE 10: Venetian milk-glass figures in an amusing procession around a potted plant. A Boston individualist uses these reproductions of 17th-century figures this way, on a wildly colorful modern cloth, at one end of her buffet luncheon table. The white primrose is in a soft spring mood. In a more zany modern spirit, they might march around a white amaryllis or an exotic plant. There are possibilities for reviving the idea of a potted plant on the table. *(Courtesy, Mrs. Isabella Grandin; photograph by Francis Lambert)*

PLATE 11: At the enchanted banquet. Beauty's father is "served by invisible hands." *(Illustration by Edmund Dulac for* Beauty and the Beast *from* The Sleeping Beauty and Other Fairy Tales, *by Sir Arthur Quiller-Couch, ed., London:* c. *1910)*

❧ TWO

The Conversation Piece

THERE CAN never have been a time when a clever host or hostess did not appreciate the value of a "conversation piece" to get a party off to a good start and to make it memorable. In every century the basic ingredients of a successful conversation piece are the same: surprise, imagination, and immediacy. Whatever the surprise, it must be presented with flair, but skillful timing is perhaps the most important factor. The conversation piece must come at the exact moment when the traditional way of doing things has lost its meaning, its practicality, or even its appeal. In other words it must strike a responsive note in its particular environment in order to live up to its name—to be, in fact, worth talking about.

Today we are more apt to respond to understatement than to magnificence and to individuality rather than to formal elegance. We tend to reject the 19th-century preoccupation with the "correct" and consequently often take pleasure in the daring or the unconventional. If something "different" can be achieved in a relaxed and effortless way, our admiration knows no bounds.

Success may come simply because the exigencies of a unique situation have been met with individuality and aplomb. Recently a flower show was held on a day so hot that the hostess for the judges' luncheon felt, herself, rather like a wilted flower. But a centerpiece had to be provided for the table and it had to be *good*. When the guests came into the dining room expecting to see just another flower arrangement, there was a unanimous exclamation of pleasure.

They were charmed with the simplicity and the delightfully cool effect of fresh lemons inside a large and beautiful covered dish of Waterford glass, their fragrance from recent handling still lingering in the air. Admired as much as the refreshing, crisp centerpiece was the way in which the hostess herself had managed to keep cool.

With almost as little effort, and with unexpectedly simple materials, another present-day hostess provided a brilliant table setting worthy of the drama and high style of the 17th century. At a really "smashing" party to wind up the summer season at Nantucket Island, great silver salvers at each end of the buffet table were centered by huge purple cabbages scooped out for cocktail sauce and their leaves opened to make petal cups for pink shrimp, lobster meat, and other hors d'œuvre. The tablecloth was pink damask, and the centerpiece lavish with rubrum lilies and garden flowers in pinks, lavenders, and purples. Derek Clifford, in *A History of Garden Design,* remarks that the major purpose of Le Nôtre's design for Fouquet's 17th-century garden at Vaux le Vicomte, was "to stun, not to charm," and thus perfectly expressed the spirit of the "Splendid Century." This 20th-century table at Nantucket evoked the same dramatic mood and managed not only to "stun" but, through the added seduction of color, to charm as well.

Other occasions present other possibilities. Sometimes a new material is introduced, creating a sensation. In the 15th century exquisite Venetian glass appeared with jewel-like, incredibly fragile candelabra, tall footed dishes for fruit, wine glasses, and the rest. The stems were "balustered, winged, crested with glass of another color, twisted and ringed in endless variety" (Plate 13), as N. Hudson Moore, author of *Old Glass* describes them. Everyone talked of these marvelous things, and soon all over Europe glass factories were making glass *façon de Venise.*

Again, in the 18th century, when porcelain was first made in Europe, perfectly suiting rococo taste with its gleaming surface and rhythmic contours, a whole range of fresh ideas for table ornaments was opened up.

Any new art form may claim attention. The owner of a very modern house surprised her guests not long ago by attaching roses in tiny glass tubes to a mobile suspended above the dinner table. It was both practical and imaginative as she not only wanted to be avant-garde but needed to save space on the surface of the table. However, it was not really a new idea, as she may have thought, for in *Le Cannameliste Français* by Gilliers, Chef d'Office to the King of Poland in the 18th century, it is suggested that grapes "are most advantageous hung in the air, attached by a thread either from a suspended hoop or from an ornamental nail."[1]

A still older device to evoke delight is the introduction of a touch of humor or wit in the presentation of food. Picture how Pliny's guests must have marveled when invited to sup in his garden. Their wonderment began when they seated themselves on a marble bench under an arbor and the pressure of their weight caused the water to gush forth from beneath the bench into the pool, yet never to fill it to overflowing. This introduction put the guests into a fine mood for whimsey, and when the meal appeared the tray of appetizers and the larger dishes were placed around the margin of the pool while the smaller ones in the form of little ships and waterfowl swam in the water (Plate 12). As Pliny well realized in the 1st century A.D., informality can be conveyed by unexpected and humorous innovations.

On the other hand, Oriental surprises were more solemn and were apt to be mingled with a sense of mystery and awe. At a banquet at the court of the Great Khan in the 13th century, Marco Polo was fascinated, and a little frightened, by the mysterious way in which the court "enchanters and astrologers . . . caused the cups to move from their places . . . without being touched . . . and present themselves to the Emperor."[2]

Mechanical inventions had an appeal in those early days which is difficult for us to appreciate. Marvelous as we know our 20th-century electronic gadgets to be, they are so ubiquitous that they seem quite commonplace. The electric eye that opens the door of the supermarket for us is not looked upon as a marvel or as something supernatural but simply as a convenience. But to Marco Polo the fantastic machines of the Great Khan seemed almost akin to necromancy.

In the East such devices were, even then, an ancient tradition dating back to the days of Heron of Alexandria whose inventions in the 2nd or 3rd century were operated by water, steam, compressed air, or delicately adjusted weights and counterweights. His writings were translated by the Arabs and the Persians, and in this way his secrets spread throughout Asia and Asia Minor where extravagantly fanciful "machines" were observed by many travelers long before Marco Polo.

In Bagdad in the 10th century, according to Marie Gothein, ambassadors from Byzantium saw an amazing tree with gold and silver leaves hung with jeweled fruits. On the branches sat birds also made of silver and gold, "and when a breeze passed through they whistled and sighed in a wonderful way." In Constantinople the Emperor Constantine VII had a magnificent throne that might be lowered and raised at will. It was guarded by huge gilded lions which could be made to beat on the ground with their tails and open their jaws and roar. Here also was a metal tree, gold plated, with gilt birds of many sizes which "sang, each with its proper notes."

European Crusaders, traveling adventurers, and invading Franks saw these extraordinary machines and brought their secrets home in the Middle Ages to delight kings and princes eager to astonish their guests at great feasts and entertainments. Wonderful indeed, in the 15th century, were the fantastic mechanized animals which enlivened the wedding banquet of Charles the Bold, Duke of Burgundy, as described by the duke's chronicler, Olivier de La Marche. And equally mysterious and exciting were the elaborate table fountains dispends jets of wine or rose water at the same banquet (Plate 14).

Other objects on the Medieval and Renaissance table were occasionally mechanized, including the richly ornamented receptacle known as a nef which every king and prince of the blood then displayed on his table (Plate 15) to hold his condiments, personal utensils, and various charms believed to have the power of detecting poison. This ornament was always shaped more or less like a ship, (nef being originally an early French word for ship), and it symbolized good fortune and fair sailing on the uncertain seas of Life.

A remarkable nef said to have belonged to the Emperor Charles V was not only an elaborate example of the goldsmith's art but also was fully mechanized. It represented a royal ship, more literally than the rather vaguely suggested ship-form of earlier nefs, and was complete with sailors manipulating the rigging, musicians playing various instruments, and a group of courtiers bowing obsequiously before the emperor. This nef still exists and is now in the Cluny Museum in Paris. Recently, for the entertainment of an international gathering of clockmakers, it was set in motion, its intricate mechanism still in working condition (Plate 16)!

It is clear that European engineers soon rivaled the "crafty enchanters" of the Great Khan. Guests at royal banquets in Europe were now astonished by all sorts of mechanical surprises. The most spectacular of these were the "flying tables," sections of the dining table which descended from the opened ceiling, bringing down and later removing the platters and other requirements for each course, including decorations of "precious stones, mirrors, and other things to delight the eye."

Le Grand d'Aussy, who devotes several pages to the subject of these fantastic "machines,"[3] reports that at one of the Duke of Burgundy's banquets in

1453, "the different services . . . came down from the ceiling in chariots painted in gold or in blue, and then were carried away in the same manner." He tells us that Brantôme (1535–1614) describes a similar feast where the ceiling, painted to represent the sky, opened up to give passage to "machines in the form of clouds." At dessert there was an artificial storm, letting fall a rain of sweet smelling water and a hail of *dragées* which were sugared almonds or similar confections. Sometimes *dragées* contained pistachios, aniseed, coriander, or were filled with liqueurs. Made in fantastic shapes of men, women, and beasts, they were vastly admired.

When Marie de Medici, daughter of the Grand Duke of Tuscany, was betrothed to Henry IV of France in 1600, there was a superb feast with a table which parted in two and was taken away while another table rose from below laden with all sorts of fruits for the dessert, and at a great banquet given for the English King, Charles II, at which the French ambassador was present, "everything came down in clouds." This flying table may have been accompanied by thunder, easily managed by releasing wooden balls down a series of inclined planes inside a cylinder, a device which according to Chapuis goes back to Heron of Alexandria. Rain was usually represented by a light sprinkle of rose water.

Royalty was quick to see the advantage of "flying tables," as under these circumstances only a few trusted servants were needed in immediate attendance. Russia, with a court notorious for its intrigue, made use of this contrivance early in the 18th century at the first "Hermitage" built by Peter the Great at Peterhof. Later, the Empress Elizabeth had one installed at another "Hermitage," a charming retreat in the garden at Tsarskoë Selo, which Rastrelli designed for her in 1752. This provided a perfect place for entertaining foreign dignitaries as well as for intimate suppers. Although her successor, Catherine the Great, preferred classic taste to the rococo style of this enchanting pavilion, she too, no doubt, appreciated the advantage of its five dinner tables, in the central domed saloon and the four ante rooms, each table fitted with machinery for lowering the individual plates and dishes. At the pull of a string, these disappeared through the floor to the kitchen below to be dealt with according to a guest's order, which he had only to write on the little slate attached. When the meal was over, all the tables were lowered bodily. A neat section of parquetry covered each opening; magically, the supper room was ready for dancing.[4]

Mme. du Barry's "flying table" at the Petit Trianon (designed by Loriot in 1769 and considered superior to a rather balky one Mme. de Pompadour had used at Choisy) also went below through a trap door, and the opening was covered between courses by beautiful metal leaves centered by a rose. In another room at the Petit Trianon was a round table bearing a series of mobile plateaux which could be changed in size according to the number of the guests.

Naturally everyone could not afford such "fairy-like magnificences," but simpler mechanical devices were created for less affluent tables. Vaucanson, a clever 18th-century mechanician, was a famous maker of *automates,* and everyone admired his spirited flute player and his amazing mechanical duck which waddled from one end of the table to the other to astonish guests with its amusing and lifelike performance. Eighteenth-century dessert centerpieces of porcelain or silver-gilt sometimes included dancing figures or little concealed music boxes, "playing airs lasting a half an hour." Whenever new versions of the mechanical surprise appeared, they created a stir and the success of the party was assured.

Fantastic figures made of pastry or sugar paste were another form of centerpiece featured at desserts. These were not mechanical but were most decorative and provided novelty and amusement.

Germany has been credited with the introduction of this fashion in the 15th century, but *The Accomplisht Cook,* written in 1685, claims that according to Plutarch they go back to the days of Lucullus (110–56 B.C.) who had every day on his table "fine dainty dishes, with works of pastry, banketting dishes and fruit curiously wrought and prepared." If this ancient custom was revived in 15th-century Germany, it spread very quickly, for *The Noble Boke off Cookry,* written in England shortly after Neville's feast in 1467, describes the "crown-açon" (coronation) banquet of Henry V in 1413 as having "suttletes in pastry and sugar" and "Egillis [eagles] of gold displayde for suttletes with a scripture in their billes."

These curious sugar figures of men, women, birds, animals, castles, and heraldic devices (Plate 19) were known in England as "suttletes" (or sutteltes) and "conceipts." They were molded of jellies or almond paste, frequently "gilded" with saffron or yolk of egg. They seem to have been made chiefly for decoration, not to be eaten at least until after the party when they were given to important guests as souvenirs of the occasion.[5] So beloved were sugar ornaments that they continued to be in fashion for several centuries, varying in form according to changing taste and increasing sophistication (Plates 20 and 21).

In the Middle Ages people, loving pageantry, loud unexpected noises, and low comedy, were easily pleased by things which to us seem rather childish. We learn from Robert May's *The Accomplisht Cook* that some of their sugar ornaments were practical jokes such as live frogs baked in a pie "to make the ladies skip and shreek." This must surely have been the origin of the four and twenty blackbirds baked in a pie of the nursery rhyme or of Jack Horner's pie, still popular at childrens' parties.

Another favorite medieval joke, he tells us, was a stag of pastry filled with claret wine, so made that when an arrow was withdrawn from its side, the wine gushed forth like blood from a wound. Still another was a castle of sugar paste with tiny guns in the turrets filled with real gunpowder. At a given signal the guns would be set off to salute the guest of honor, and the ladies, given blown egg shells filled with rose water, would "storm the castle in frolic."

Not all sugar ornaments, however, furnished childish amusement. Many of them were purely decorative, placed as accents among the fruits constituting the dessert. Amazement and admiration greeted them for the cleverness with which they were made and they became more and more elaborate as time went on.

During the Renaissance coarse jokes were gradually discarded, and the sugar figures took a religious turn or were, perhaps, allegorical or representative of classic gods or goddesses and other mythological characters. Sometimes a complete allegory was presented in a series of figures down the center of the table with a flattering, and quite obvious, allusion to the godlike qualities of a reigning prince or visiting potentate.

In Italy in the 17th century, historical figures were the thing, and with typical baroque grandeur, they were "half as big as the Life" and "modeled to the utmost skill of a statuary." At a banquet given by the British Ambassador in Rome in 1687 these *trionfi* (triumphs), as the Italians called them, were ranged down the center of an eight-foot wide table "to gratify the Eye, as the Meats, Musique and Perfumes do the other Senses."[6]

Fascinating side lights on this banquet and on the one given by Pope Clement IX for Queen Christina of Sweden (Plate 21) are given in a lively article by Georgina Masson in the English magazine, *Apollo* (May, 1966), in which she tells us that records of craftsmen's accounts still preserved in the State Archives at Rome give the amounts paid to specific artists who designed the *trionfi* for these and other banquets, to the sculptors who made the molds for them of wood or gesso, and to the lesser artisans who cast them in sugar and gilded them with gold leaf.

By the 18th century sugar ornaments were more a traditional form of decoration than a novelty, but any new presentation of them still seems to have attracted attention. The most exciting and completely fresh interpretation of the now familiar "images" appeared in the early 18th century when these figures were translated into a wonderful new medium. Instead of sugar, they could now be made of a far more beautiful and durable material, the new European porcelain, the true secret of which had at last been discovered at Meissen in Germany (Plate 17). This fashion so captivated European society that by mid-18th century Horace Walpole, that indefatigable English letter-writer and self-appointed arbiter of taste, reported: "jellies, biscuits, sugar plombs and creams have long given way to harlequins, gondoliers, Turks, Chinese and shepherdesses of Saxon china."[7]

But what of those who could not afford this porcelain, which was both expensive and desirable, and yet wanted to be in fashion? For them confectioners now produced similar sugar ornaments made to look as much like the porcelain ones as possible (Plate 23). Instead of the old allegorical or historical figures, they made the figurines in the new rococo characterizations so charmingly portrayed in porcelain and experimented with mixtures of dough, talc, and tragacanth gum to more nearly resemble biscuit porcelain.

Confectioners also made delightful little scenes for the dessert plateau, another popular type of table decoration in the 18th century. (Today's interpretation of this idea is seen in Plate 18.) There might be little figures skating or dancing, or perhaps scenes from well-known operas or ballets. Theater-mad society would instantly recognize favorite performers or characters from the *commedia dell' arte* (Plate 22). In France one confectioner, alas, tried to represent a snow scene by adding ground glass to the sugar coating of his confections, but the tragic consequences when some of these were inadvertently eaten made necessary a royal decree forbidding their production. A rival soon invented a more innocuous substance which not only gave the desired sparkle of frost (glitter, in any form, was irresistible) but also provided that darling of the 18th century, a "transformation scene" in which the sugar coating melted with the heat of the room just enough to transform a winter scene into spring! This was an instantaneous success, but it is reported that the secret unfortunately died with the inventor.[8]

These little scenes, of course, were sometimes made of other materials. For the wealthy there was the new porcelain or there were the equally charming glass figures from Nevers. Less expensive miniatures were made of wood, wax, metal, or even of osier twigs. An old pattern book for basket-makers shows designs for little thatched barns and cottages, with wheelbarrows and other implements for the plateau, listed under the heading of "Adult Toys" (Fig. 5).

FIGURE 5: A basketry well-sweep. This is part of a table group of "Adult Toys" showing Marie Antoinette's little "Farm," probably a 19th-century version. *(Courtesy, Williams-Sonoma, San Francisco, California; sketch by Bentson)*

These are said to be replicas of Marie Antoinette's little "Farm" in the park at the Petit Trianon where she and her ladies tried to escape from the boredom and formality of court routine by playing at gardening and dairying. In a Paris basket shop not long ago, a San Francisco importer discovered an amusing little thatch-roofed wellhead from one of these groups, with a ladder hung at a rakish angle among vines bearing artificial fruits and vegetables. Figures to animate such little scenes were dressed in appropriate costumes and set on the plateau surrounded by artificial flowers and trees.

The transition between the rococo forms of the earlier 18th century and the classic style of the late 18th and early 19th centuries is amazingly abrupt. Change was always welcome to break the monotony of court etiquette, but this particular change was unusually exciting because it was so sudden and so complete. Almost overnight straight lines replaced curves, and sobriety took the place of exuberance. It was not even fashionable any more to be gay! A smile was considered to have more *ton* than "vulgar" laughter. Coming at a time when the wayward curve, however charming, had begun to pall, the new style, fashioned on inspirations of Greek and Roman art and sparked by the recent excavations of Roman antiquities at Herculaneum and Pompeii, was accepted with open arms. Even such minor arts as table decoration soon reflected the trend.

So we see both porcelain and sugar ornaments toward the end of the 18th century becoming soberly and severely classic in contrast to the gay and light-hearted rococo. Gone are the vivacious figures in crinoline, the amorous youths, and the merry shepherdesses. Instead we now have Pomona, goddess of the fruits of autumn, standing serenely in the shelter of a miniature Greek temple surrounded by her attendant goddesses, or perhaps a group of Muses on "Mt. Parnassus" dominating the center of the table, whether in porcelain or sugar paste. By way of a mechanical surprise, Pomona's porcelain temple might have a "secret artifice" in the dome which contains water to be released to run down inside the columns into the base of the plateau and bounce up as little fountains in a miniature garden parterre (Plate 24).

This fashion for a make-believe garden on the plateau, long a favored centerpiece idea, must of course conform to whatever type of garden is momentarily in vogue. The baroque and rococo "embroidered parterre" is followed by the classic formal garden, only to be supplanted in the early 19th century by the English naturalistic romantic garden employing "whole meadows of china cattle," artificial grass, gravel paths, and winding streams in which real goldfish "glister" to amaze the company.

As inspiration for the naturalistic garden came from China, it is not surprising that Chinese pagodas and other garden details of Oriental persuasion, which had delighted the early 18th century, did not lose their appeal in spite of the vogue for classicism. Since real gardens of this period often had Oriental features, it follows that these same features would appear on the table. Early 19th-century cookbooks tell how to cover tin molds in the form of a Chinese temple or how to border walks of "shot comfits" with a Chinese railing of baked paste, often in combination with a classic parterre!

Chinese detail, even today, seems to introduce a note of the exotic, a touch of theater that is irresistible. Often it enlivens the severity of a modern design just as it apparently afforded relief from stark classicism during the Classic Revival. It has been suggested that some 18th-century artists, even the strictest classicists, occasionally used chinoiserie as a "pretext for playing," an escape into a dream country where all liberties might be permitted in contrast to the arbitrary rules of antique art to which they adhered devotedly in more serious endeavors. Chinese design may still retain for us a bit of that early fantasy.

Even though we may smile at some of the curious devices which amused and delighted people in other days, we are not by any means immune to flights of fancy, to a "secret artifice" or an "agreeable surprise." What is pleasing to us may differ from what was appealing in another age. We are not intrigued by the idea of live frogs in a pie and we have little occasion for wine fountains or flying tables, but many of the things we enjoy today are actually a reflection of some custom or convention of table decoration which goes back for centuries. Swans, ships, mermaids, or other figures carved in ice, which are occasionally seen today on the buffet at a fashionable hotel or exclusive club to hold the hors d'œuvre, are only a modern version of the "suttletes" of the Middle Ages. G. Mourey in *Le Livre des Fêtes Françaises* tells of similar fantasies in the 18th century when the buffet held "vases made of ice of differing shapes and sizes through the transparency of which one could see the flowers and fruits which they contained."[9]

At the beginning of the 20th century the practice of serving ice cream in amusing forms resting in spun sugar was a standard feature of a child's birthday party. This is a treat rarely seen today, but at a recent Valentine's Day fashion-show luncheon at a hotel, the guests, adults, were greeted at dessert by heart-shaped molds of strawberry ice cream in nests of spun sugar, a "conceipt" old enough to be new to a whole generation which had never seen such delights. The pewter molds in which birds, animals, fruits, and other ice cream forms were once made by caterers in immense quantities are now items of whimsey at the antique shop. Who would guess that ice-cream hearts in spun sugar are descended from Lucullan dishes "curiously wrought and prepared" and that the familiar treat of fifty years ago has again become a conversation piece?

Other early table surprises frequently appear in a new guise. At a recent Christmas party young and old alike were as much charmed by a tiny "tree" of eucalyptus leaves revolving on a music box ornamented with gay paper cutouts in the manner of old French *découpage* as 18th-century guests must have been by a porcelain music box playing tunes lasting half an hour. A 1965 magazine article showing several tables imaginatively decorated with glass balls, chunks of rough glass, or a collection of antique glass paperweights to create "dancing lights at a party" gives only a fresh and delightful version of the decorations at a great fete at 17th-century Versailles, when there were, between vases of flowers, "balls of crystal on which the light was refracted, making the effect of the rainbow."[10]

Above another contemporary holiday table white *origami* (paper) doves fluttered in a delicate mobile, reminiscent of a 17th-century flying plateau which, as a final flourish at the end of the meal, displayed "the gardens of Alcinous" and released "many small [live] birds flying all around the room."

A word of warning—taste and restraint are needed when the fanciful is introduced. It should not degenerate into the use of tawdry Santas and Disneyana from the ten-cent store. Our own inventions, whether inspired by historic examples or modern art, will have more distinction. Modern versions of old ideas may be simple devices, easily achieved given a little talent and imagination (Plates 25 and 26), or they may be elaborate and extravagant, not just amusing but spectacular.

Garden Club of America judges at the 1950 New York Flower Show were entertained at a sunset champagne party in a famous designer's penthouse apartment at the top of Rockefeller Center. The high-ceilinged room was long and narrow, all glass on three sides, but the end windows with bamboo blinds tempered their superb view. The nearby tall buildings thus veiled had the effect of a tapestry or a mural, even more beautiful than the broad panorama of the city on either side of the room. As the setting sun touched the rivers, turning them into bright metallic ribbons of light, clouds of pink and gold drifted in and out around the tops of the skyscrapers. The guests watched the glowing spectacle until the first lights came on, winking through the now darkening screen at the end of the room. Suddenly symphonic music filled the air, issuing from hidden loud speakers ingeniously contrived to heighten the dramatic moment, and not even the enchanters and astrologers of Kublai Khan could have produced a greater marvel.

There is no need for us to scorn flying tables, whistling golden birds, and the automata which furnished table surprises in the past, even if 17th-century purists deplored them as "grotesques suitable to amuse an age incapable of any occupation more serious." We are equally susceptible to present-day fantasies and extravagances, proving the wisdom and wit of mischievous La Fontaine who said in *Les Automates:* "*Le monde est vieux, cependent, / Il le faut amuser encor comme un enfant.*" (The world is old, nevertheless, / Like a child, it must still be amused.)

PLATE 12: Straw swan with hors d'œuvre. The setting suggests a river motif for the presentation of the hors d'œuvre, or it would be charming for a summer party beside the pool. A wooden tray in fish shape holds Mexican tacos garnished with water-cress, and goldfish crackers are in a wooden bowl. Wavy lines on the ice bucket and on the border of the tortoise-shell patterned plate carry out the theme to make a conversation piece for the cocktail hour. *(Setting by the author; photograph by Francis Lambert)*

PLATE 13: Dragon-stem goblet of Venetian glass of late 16th century. *(Corning Museum of Glass, New York)*

PLATE 14: A spectacular wine fountain used at the Burgundian court in the late 14th century. Made of silver gilt and translucent enamel, this 12½″ ×9½″ piece exhibits the skill and imagination of the goldsmith. *(Cleveland Museum of Art; gift of J. H. Wade)*

PLATE 15: The Duc de Berry at table, and his magnificent
nef, 15th century. *(From a 15th-century book of hours,* Les Très
Riches Heures du Duc de Berry, *painted by P. de Limbourg;
courtesy, Musée de Condé, Chantilly)*

PLATE 16: A mechanized nef of silver gilt. This piece is said to have belonged to the Emperor Charles V, and was made in Germany in the 16th century. When set in motion its sailors manipulate the rigging, and on the deck, musicians play their instruments and courtiers bow before the emperor. *(Cluny Museum, Paris)*

PLATE 17: Triton, by Kaëndler; Meissen porcelain, Germany, *c.* 1750. No doubt part of a centerpiece group surrounding Neptune or a river god, this figure shows a fluid rhythm and monumental character. *(Museum of Fine Arts, Boston)*

PLATE 18: Images of sugar. Made by a confectioner today, these figures prove that skill in the art is still available. *(Christmas setting by the author; photograph by Francis Lambert)*

PLATE 19: "Suttletes" and "conceipts," displayed for a banquet in Germany in the 15th century. This affair seems to be so elaborate that it was set up in another room and guests are admiring it in amazement, as they well might. (The artist's sense of scale must have been at fault for this table, in relation to the figures, would have been at least twelve feet wide!) The fantastic variety of sugar ornaments in the shape of birds, animals, castles, trees, and heraldic devices gives an idea of the ingenuity of the 15th-century confectioner. *(From* Deutsches Leben der Vergangenheit in Bildern *by E. Diederichs, Jena, 1908)*

PLATE 20: Confectioner's mold for the figure of St. Catherine, 15th century. *(Courtesy, Trustees of the London Museum)*

PLATE 21: Religious subjects. These were the figures displayed on the table at a banquet given in Rome in 1668 by Pope Clement IX in honor of Queen Christina of Sweden. *(Nationalmuseum, Stockholm)*

PLATE 22: Porcelain figure by Bustelli, master modeler of the Nymphenburg factory. It represents a character from the popular Italian Comedy which toured Europe in the 18th century. George Savage says of Bustelli, "His art is sensitive, elegant, full of life, and of a movement which has been forever crystalized at its most significant point." This figure appears to be arrested in the middle of a spirited pirouette. *c.* 1760. *(Metropolitan Museum of Art; gift of R. Thornton Wilson, 1950, in memory of Florence Ellsworth Wilson)*

PLATE 23: Eighteenth-century sugar flowers. Realistic flowers of sugar being made by this group shown in a French cookbook of 1751, *Le Cannameliste Français*. When finished, the sugar flowers were arranged in vases for the dessert plateau, as shown at the bottom of the page. They were also used to ornament the tops of pyramids of dried fruits or "to make a Nosegay for the middle of your Desert, or they may be laid in order in a Basket. . . . If they are tied up in a Bunch, a Foot or Stock may be made of Marchpane, roll'd out and wreathed, after the same manner as Nosegays . . ." *(Courtesy, Harvard College Library)*

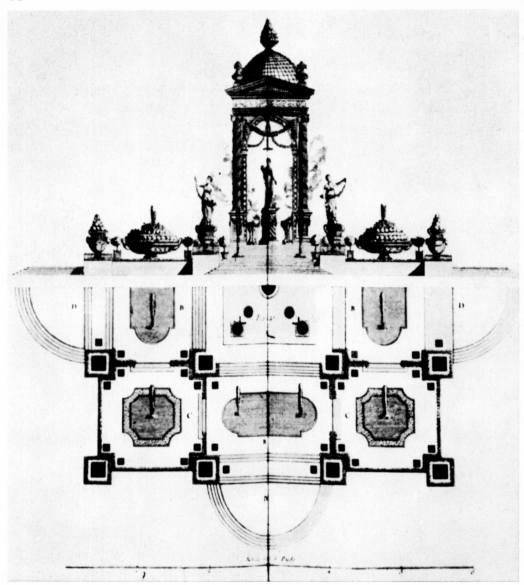

PLATE 24: Diagram for a surtout-de-table, late 18th century. In the form of a garden parterre, this diagram shows the elevation and one-half the plan. The temple in the center, dedicated to Pomona, had a secret artifice in the dome. The centerpiece could be used as a whole or in part, depending upon the size and importance of the party. (*A Classic Revival design of the late 18th century from Diderot's* Encyclopédie)

PLATE 25: Christmas centerpiece. A problem often encountered today is to make a conversation piece for a large gathering of some special group at a hotel or club. This Travel Club's Christmas party featured mid-century lilies in an exotic wood burl, combined with shells from faraway beaches. Arranged in the shells are the strange, velvety leaves of Kalanchoë beharensis, studded with Christmas balls. *(Arrangement by Mrs. William White Howells; photograph by David Lawson)*

PLATE 26: A table for a musical party. The modern musical theme was designed by the well-known French musicians, Henri Sauget and Georges Auric (Director of the Paris Opera), whose portraits by Mme. Auric appear on the wall above. This table was one of a group of table settings designed by modern painters, poets, musicians, and sculptors at an exhibition chez Christofle, the famous French silversmiths. Invisible wires hold the musical instruments and musical scores in a lively and amusing grouping, and the musical motifs on the plates are also modern in spirit. *(Courtesy, Christofle, Paris)*

✾ THREE

Garlands, Chaplets, & Strewn Flowers

JUST AS a real garland is bound up and interwoven with flowers, foliage, and fruits, so is the word itself interwoven, through centuries of association, with ideas of dignity, ceremonial tribute, beauty, and festive grace. These traditions are so deeply imbedded in our consciousness that we sense, even if we do not know explicitly, their age-old, complex implications. When we use garlands today, whether in reverent or festive mood at our Christmas celebrations, or as an exuberant expression of the harvest's abundance at Thanksgiving, or merely to suggest the formal elegance of the 18th and 19th centuries on occasions of social importance, they still have the power to impart an added luster and warmth of feeling.

Apparently the word "garland," as well as all its European variants, did not appear until the Middle Ages, and its origin is unknown. But the idea of twining flowers together to make a rope or a wreath is an ancient custom, one which has been continuously followed among most peoples since the dawn of history and has been practiced for many reasons, whether magical, ritualistic, psychological, or social.

Bronislaw Malinowski, the great Polish anthropologist, in his study of life in Melanesia (*Argonauts of the Western Pacific,* 1922) describes the garlanding of canoes to bring magical good fortune to trading ventures. "Put on your wreath of aromatic herbs and fly!" says the voyager to his craft. Himself he anoints with coconut oil and mint, and he wears a wreath of the white, wonderfully scented *butia* flowers in order to be irresistibly attractive—this was his magic. Not only in Melanesia was faith in the efficacy of fragrances persistent, but in other lands and other times as well aromas were believed to purify the air, repel disease, alert the mind, give courage to the spirit, and have a magical power to delight.

Such beliefs led naturally to the association of herbs and flowers with food to promote health and pleasure, and thus to the use of strewn flowers on the table and to the idea of providing guests at banquets with fragrant wreaths to wear. These customs continued through the Renaissance as the usual accompaniment to a meal.

There were, of course, other meanings beyond health and pleasure interwoven in the word "garland." Certain flowers were associated with specific gods, chosen as offerings to conciliate them with chaplets and garlands heaped upon their altars or images, or worn by their devotees. The association of laurel with Apollo determined the wreaths of laurel given to winners of games in his honor and the wreaths for poets whom he was thought to have divinely inspired. Garlands for winners of musical contests at rites for Athena were of gold. Perhaps the wreaths with which these honored people were crowned symbolized a kinglike importance and achievement. Or it may have been the other way around; perhaps the king's crown derived from the wreath. A proud king may have desired a richer and more princely circlet than one of humble flowers and ordered one made of precious metal, set with jewels to proclaim his sovereignty.

Be that as it may, most early wreaths were of flowers or foliage, and lists of appropriate plants and occasions suitable for the giving or wearing of wreaths found in classical literature would fill more than one sizeable volume.

The making of garlands was an established trade in ancient Greece and Rome, and garlands were often sold on contract for the year.[1] The garland sellers portrayed in Pompeian frescoes bring their wares into town in panniers on goatback and spread the garlands out for display in flower stalls (Plate 27). The role of garland maker is still important today on the islands of the Pacific and in India, Egypt, and Southeast Asia where garlands may be purchased at street markets or in shops as gifts or to welcome visitors. Pictures of Asian and Near East leaders bestowing necklaces of flowers upon visiting potentates have frequently appeared in our magazines and newsreels, and travelers to Hawaii and other Pacific islands are traditionally honored with exotic, fragrant leis on their arrival and departure. It is fascinating to note the persistence of the tradition and the way that each era and each country follows the same basic connotations.

The sprig of parsley or water cress beside the meat to glamorize a serving dish, or a bit of lemon verbena or mint on a slice of melon today is a vestige of the idea of strewn flowers, an idea inherited from the ancients who scattered herbs or flowers not only on their food but on the table and on the floor. It is known that in winter the Romans imported roses from Egypt for a single banquet.[2] Not only did they strew blossoms or petals on the table in a lavish, casual way, but as Stobart tells us in *The Grandeur That Was Rome,* at some of Nero's feasts in his palace, the Domus Aurea (Golden House), the compartments of the vaulted ceilings—inlaid with ivory—were made to revolve and scatter perfume and flowers on the guests.

During the Dark Ages, when the violence and insecurity of the times and the general lack of amenities in everyday life gave people little occasion for luxury, the use of wreaths and garlands was almost lost sight of. Certain ancient customs also, of course, were avoided in the early Christian era because of their association with pagan rites. Strewn flowers and herbs, however, continued to be used since they were considered repellent to disease, and other ceremonial traditions involving flowers were kept alive by a few sensitive people who clung to them whenever possible because they loved them and, perhaps, secretly cherished a belief in their magic power.

Fortunatus, Bishop of Poitiers in the 6th century, describes a banquet given by Rhadegund, a royal lady who had established a nunnery near Poitiers as a retreat from the dissolute life of the Merovingian court. At this banquet Fortunatus says that the floor was strewn "with so many flowers that one seemed to be walking in an enameled meadow," and "the dishes [were] wreathed, while garlands hung on the refectory walls in the manner of the Ancients." "As for the table," he continues, "it offered more roses than an entire field. The dishes reposed directly upon the roses. Instead of a linen cloth one had preferred to cover the table completely with something fragrant and agreeable."[3]

Others, too, must have cherished these customs, for there is abundant evidence that flowers were used in this way during the Middle Ages and the Renaissance. "The Goodman of Paris" in the 14th century took care to instruct his wife (who because of her extreme youth and the early loss of her parents was quite lacking in knowledge of housewifely duties) to see that greenery and violets were purchased for strewing as well as to order chaplets and garlands from the garland maker for weddings and other festivities.[4] In a list of prices paid to a Paris florist in 1498 is an item for "a great full basin of flowers to cover the table,"[5] and Aubrey, in his 17th-century *Brief Lives,* reports that at every meal Francis Lord Bacon had his table strewed with sweet herbs and flowers in season "which he sayd did refresh his spirits and memorie." (Plate 28 shows strewn flowers still appear on the table in a 17th-century painting.)

A quaint survival of this idea is sometimes encountered even today in remote country inns in France where one may sit down at luncheon and find a fresh rose or a single nasturtium laid beside each place. This custom, naïve and charming in its simplicity, is almost the age-old gesture of a friend offering a flower as a token of health, pleasure, and good will.

During the Renaissance garlands were used in many ways with delightful innovations (Fig. 6) both in the arts and in life. The pagan custom of a wreath or garland of fruits, too much beloved to be easily suppressed, was now sanctioned by the church as symbolizing the fruits of the spirit (Plate 29). Luca Della Robbia adapted the Roman fruited garland to his bas-reliefs of glazed terra cotta, surrounding his Madonnas with colorful wreaths in this new material, an innovation for architectural use which was widely admired. These reliefs are still popular, though debased by countless repetitions. However, the original works of this artist, the first member of the Della Robbia family to use this medium, are worthy of study today, as are other Renaissance garlands in various materials such as wood, bronze, and stone.

In paintings, garlands of fruit by Crivelli, Mantegna, and others, while also of Roman inspiration, have notable creative variants. Fruits, much larger in scale, are more prominently featured, and garlands of fruits and flowers, somewhat conventionalized, appear in the meander patterns of sumptuously brocaded velvets which the painters frequently used as a background for the Madonna. In such paintings, the pomegranate, pagan symbol of fruitfulness, is often shown, its meaning carried over without change into Christian symbolism.

As in the Middle Ages, Renaissance garland makers were busy providing wreaths and garlands of fresh flowers for religious festivals and also for secular occasions, proving that the roped and wreathed forms were not by any means confined to paintings or sculpture. Thomas Coryate saw these in use on holy days in Venice in 1608 and in *Coryat's Crudities,* reported them to be made of "greene leaves and fine fruits, as Melons, Oranges, Citrons, &c. . . . upon every speciall holy day in the sommer time when such things are to be had."

In Paris well into the 16th century, shops advertised chaplets of roses not only to be worn on church feast days but also to be given to banquet guests as

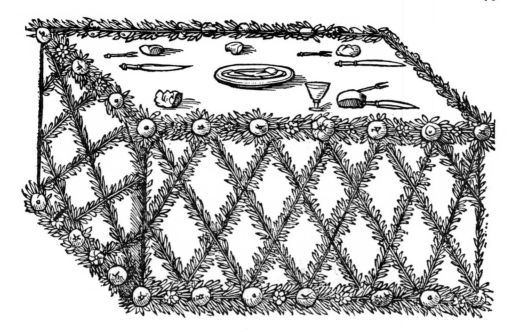

FIGURE 6: Setting at an alfresco party, 16th century. According to this table, garlands were sometimes used in a latticed pattern with a border of fruit and flowers at the top and bottom. The sparse and casual setting suggests a side table where the carving was to be done. Note the use of forks, an Italian custom which seemed very strange to Thomas Coryate, an English traveler to Italy in the 17th century. *(From* Il Trinciante, *1593; courtesy, Harvard College Library)*

well. In England the accounts of the revels at the courts of Queen Elizabeth I and King James I mentioned expenditures for "crown garlands of roses . . . base rope . . . pack thread, twyne, binding thread and needells" for garlands, as well as wages for "workfolkes the most of them being women that gathered, bownde and sorted the flowers."[6]

While in the Middle Ages and during the Renaissance guests at banquets were crowned with flowers as a matter of course (Plate 30), the only survival of this custom today seems to be the flower headdresses often worn by brides and bridesmaids as a mark of honor and importance on a festive and ceremonial occasion. The lovely "crown garlands" sometimes worn by angels in Renaissance paintings might serve as models for these and for wreaths with which to adorn our holiday tables today. Ideas for Christmas garlands can also be found in 17th- and 18th-century carvings of wood and stone. Many of the wreaths we make today have been inspired by the work of Grinling Gibbons, and with natural material such as cones, nuts, and seed pods we often simulate the fruit and flower forms carved in "lime" (linden) or fruit woods by this superb craftsman (Plate 31).

Real garlands as well as those found in architecture were lavishly displayed in the 17th century. Head stewards looped festoons around the banquet hall or twisted them around columns. Often they placed them against the tablecloth or swung them from one basket of flowers to another down the entire length of the table with typical baroque exuberance. Drama, verve, and high style marked the 17th-century garland, still following the heavy, luxuriant Roman taste in key with the "Grand Manner" prevailing at the court of Louis XIV (Plate 32). *Le Mercure* in February of 1700 reported an unusual decoration at the palace where "all the tables were covered with turf as green as if in the month of May; all were encircled with garlands charged with leaves, flowers and fruits." One wonders if these were on the new round tables made fashionable about this time by Louis XIV who hit upon this form as a clever way to defy protocol and thus place Mme. de Maintenon opposite him instead of at the far end of a long narrow table.

Christopher Marsden, in *Palmyra of the North,* describes a similar party which took place in Russia during the reign of the Empress Anne. Here, too, the tables were covered with moss, with flowers stuck in as if growing, to resemble turf banks. The guests sat on benches also made to look like turf but in this rural setting the supper, though served in country style, was actually rich and sumptuous.

In the 18th and early 19th centuries garlands were lighter, with a note of delicacy and grace more in accord with the sparkling elegance of both the rococo period and the classic revival. The two styles of garland differed only in that the rococo ones were more apt to be flung about casually and asymmetrically with an air of gaiety and abandon, whereas at the end of the 18th century, classic symmetry and precision returned to fashion.

The 18th-century vogue for garlands, almost an obsession, was prevalent not only in France but all over Europe. This fashion was adopted even in Russia in the 1730's by the Empress Anne who, Marsden says, dined under a pavilion of green silk supported by voluted pillars with wreaths of fresh flowers twisted around them.

At the marriage of the Dauphin in Paris in 1745, there were pavilions in four different parts of the city representing "The Seasons," a subject which enjoyed a great surge of popularity owing to the success of Thompson's notable poem of that name in the early 18th century. In the Spring Pavilion, silver-gilt vases ornamented with garlands of fresh flowers terminated several large buffets *au gradins* with long swags cascading down from one level to the next and spreading out on the service tables. (See Plate 35, a similar buffet *au gradins* but of the 17th century.)

Garlands of fresh flowers, however, were the exception rather than the rule at this time, particularly on the table where artificial ones seem to have been the prevailing mode. These were made in long slender chains to link together the little figures of porcelain or silver which ornamented the plateau. These "images" were occasionally modeled in graceful attitudes with their arms upraised or extended to hold the garlands in place (Plate 36).

In the late 18th and early 19th centuries, influenced by the delicate garlands of Greek inspiration made fashionable by the classic designs of Robert Adam, the festoons were reduced to threadlike strands of narrow pointed leaves accented at intervals with tiny flowers. An 1836 painting of the Waterloo Banquet (Plate 33), an event celebrated annually at Apsley House, Wellington's London residence, shows garlands of this kind. They are held by the dancing nymphs on the famed Wellington Surtout (Plate 34), an elaborate silver and gilt centerpiece presented to him by the Portuguese in 1816 in gratitude for his help in freeing Portugal from the clutches of Napoleon.

In Mexico, however, where parties were perhaps less sophisticated, garlands of fresh flowers are described by Mme. Calderon de la Barca, the English wife of the Spanish Ambassador. "The fete terminated," she says, "with the most beautiful supper I almost ever saw. A great hall was lighted with colored lamps, the walls entirely lined with green branches and hung with fresh garlands of flowers most tastefully arranged."

Garlands laid on the surface of the table in the S-curve which is familiar to us today are not mentioned, as far as can be discovered, until the late 19th century. Even then, they are chiefly reduced to flat patterns of overlapping leaves and flowers laid directly on the tablecloth and reminiscent of the Victorian "bedding out" of fashionable gardens of the day. Thomas Skelton Harrison, Diplomatic Agent and Consul of the U.S. to the Khedival court of Cairo in the 1890's, describes a garland of roses "with their stems and leaves, in the form of a continuous letter S, only sideways," on his own table at an important dinner party. It appears to have been his own idea to use a garland in this way. This gentleman filled his *Diary of a Diplomat in the East* with accounts of his own parties and of sumptuous table decorations at various other official banquets involving magnificent epergnes, silver candelabra of twelve to fifteen branches, "urns and other forms." These accounts are interspersed with fulsome descriptions of tropical plant material never exactly identified, without contributing anything of interest regarding the problems of State connected with his position! Other garlands he describes were of the Victorian flower-bed persuasion in circular, crescent, or star formation.

In spite of such minor differences of changing taste and national interpretation, the garland more than any form of table decoration has come down to us practically unaltered in appearance or connotation. It is true that we use garlands very seldom today, except at Christmas and on a few other important occasions, and this is as it should be. A garland *is* special and is universally accepted as a gesture and token of homage. It sets a mood of pomp and circumstance for which there are still opportunities even in our informal society. Perhaps it is more meaningful today than in the 18th century when the form was so ubiquitous that, charming as it was, it may have lost much of its significance.

For an October garden club dinner a few years ago, long slender garlands were made of the beautiful fan-shaped leaves of the ginkgo tree which, in autumn, turn to gold with the texture of Chinese silk. The tiny fans were thickly ruched, and their golden sheen was enhanced by the candlelight from a pair of French gilt-bronze candelabra said to have belonged to Talleyrand. The garlands trailed sinuously against the gold silk-damask cloth, swept up the candelabra and down again to meet a low centerpiece of flowers, providing a setting of appropriate elegance and distinction for an important occasion.

But homage and special tributes need not always be reserved for grand and formal gatherings. A small, intimate supper, given with more than ordinary gusto, might extol some individual achievement in literature or in the arts or celebrate the birthday of a very special person. At such a time an added gesture of allegiance and admiration might be given by adorning a candelabrum or a plaster cherub with a garland of flowers—or by fashioning a simple wreath to surround a basket of violets or lilies of the valley.

PLATE 27: Pompeiian garland sellers. They bring their wares into town and spread them out on benches or hang them on racks for sale. *(Fresco from the House of the Vettii, Pompeii; Art Reference Bureau Inc., New York)*

PLATE 28: Strewn flowers on the table in a 17th-century "Last Supper" by Jorg Ratgel. Though strewn flowers are more a medieval custom than one of the 17th century, they are clearly shown here not only on the table but also on the floor. The artist may have realized it was an ancient custom and attempted historic accuracy, but he also included 17th-century table appointments such as the gold or silver cups and fine glass goblets. The roast lamb appears to be garnished with lilies of the valley, and violets are scattered on the cloth. *(From* Les Accessoires du Costume et du Mobilier *by d'Allemagne; Paris, 1928)*

PLATE 29: Garland of fruit and foliage. This garland in Mantegna's painting, "St. George," is bound with vermilion cords, setting off the yellow and orange fruits and the green foliage. *(From the Academy, Venice; Art Reference Bureau, Inc., New York)*

PLATE 30: Banquet guests wearing wreaths at a gay party. *(The scene is taken from a German book on banquets for nobles,* Ein Neu Kochbuch, *by Rumpolt; Frankfurt, 1587; courtesy, Harvard College Library)*

PLATE 31: Christmas wreath as centerpiece. On an apricot linen damask cloth, this wood-brown wreath of natural material encircles a hand-carved wooden angel from Austria. Alternating acorns and paulownia pods are accented with beech nuts, some showing their silky, almost apricot-colored inside surface and others turned with their shaggy brown coats uppermost. The foundation of the wreath is made of individual pine-cone scales sewed to a cloth-bound octagonal wire frame. This type of wreath takes time and thought but can be put away in a box and used many times, becoming a beloved feature of the family Christmas. *(Wreath made by the author over twenty years ago; photograph by Francis Lambert)*

PLATE 32: Flower garlands, 1707. These Venetian garlands decorate a gay carnival pavilion in a painting by Rudolph Byss.
Musicians perform behind the buffet: guests are seated at a small
table at the other end of the pavilion, not shown here (see Plate
49). *(Detail from* "The Carnival in Venice," *by Rudolph Byss,* c.
1707; courtesy, Wadsworth Athenaeum, Hartford)

PLATE 33: Detail of the painting, "The Waterloo Banquet for 1836," by William Salter. The event was held annually at Wellington's town house (Apsley House, London). On the table is the famed Wellington Surtout presented to Wellington by the Portuguese government. *(Wellington Museum, London; Crown Copyright)*

PLATE 34: Section of the Wellington Surtout. This detail shows some of the nymphs which were originally intended to hold garlands (as shown in Plate 33). Later the wreaths on their heads were placed in their hands instead to eliminate the need for garlands. *(Wellington Museum, London; Crown Copyright)*

PLATE 35: Buffet au gradins at Versailles in the 17th century. Here is an affair replete with garlands, draped candelabra, and chandeliers. Sweetmeats and pyramids of fruit make a sumptuous dessert. Sculptured cupids preside over a fountain, perhaps for wine or rose water. *(From* Les Plaisirs de l'Isle Enchantée, *a 1674 fete book; courtesy, Harvard College Library)*

PLATE 36: Two silver-gilt figures by French silversmith Nicholas Cousinet, made for the Portuguese court, 1757–58. They represent a French couple and are part of a set of sixteen figures for the banquet table, with a man and woman for each of eight countries. The hands of the figures are upraised in different attitudes to hold garlands. The set originally included a matching plateau and candelabra. *(National Museum of Antique Art, Lisbon)*

❧ FOUR

Flowers on the Table & Nearby

IN EVERY century, our own included, fashions in flowers for the table are always, logically enough, closely related to other prevailing tastes and customs. The arrangements of lotus set out in low bowls among the meats and piles of fruit at a banquet in ancient Egypt were formal and highly stylized as was all Egyptian design. Today, because we enjoy stylization and associate it with modern art, Egyptian flower designs appeal to us and seem appropriate in modern settings. Thus a style which was "right" for the Egyptians has come full circle and could be "right" for us, though it would have been "wrong" according to the emotional and romantic preferences of the Victorians.

Medieval fashions, though nearer to us in time, seem more remote. But to appreciate the naïve pleasure that people in the Middle Ages found in strewn flowers on the dining table, one has only to look at the little flowers that medieval artists and craftsmen faithfully and lovingly portrayed (Plates 39 and 40), whether carved in stone, painted in illuminated manuscripts, or woven in tapestries. They are so intimately and exactly observed that they stand out with a startling clarity, taking on an almost uncanny, magic quality. In *Great Flower Books,* Sacheverell Sitwell, with his rare gift for discerning the inner nature of things, makes it clear that "to the Medieval painter the strawberry, like the carnation and the periwinkle, was a thing to wonder at." He reiterates the thought in the following perceptive sentence: "Though the individual buttercup be but a golden item, a stitch, as it were, in a meadow of cloth of gold, it is, yet, a golden cup or grail, and the eyes dazzle on looking into its golden circumference and at the shine and glitter of its metal." Considered in this spirit of reverence and wondering affection, we can understand why people were content to enjoy flowers just as they were, without artifice.

Of course garlands were arranged more formally and made with professional skill, following a more sophisticated custom inherited from the ancients, and at splendid feasts in the late Middle Ages there were occasional elaborate centerpieces including flowers. At a banquet given in 1455 by the Count du Maine, brother-in-law to Charles VII, there was a centerpiece representing a flowery green meadow with a tower in the middle which was a cage for singing birds. Peacock feathers were added for good measure, and banners with the arms of the Count and of his particularly honored guests fluttered gaily from the miniature tower's battlements (Plate 41).[1] Centerpieces like this, as well as garlands, were for important personages and great occasions. But anyone could enjoy the fragrance and charm of violets or other simple flowers of field or garden, whether strewn on the tablecloth or thrust casually into a jam pot or apothecary jar for longer lasting pleasure, as they are in the 15th-century painting by the Master of Frankfurt of "The Painter and His Wife" (Plate 42).

Today we no longer scatter flowers on the table in medieval fashion because our 20th-century sense of design and our inherited Victorian conventions relating to what is "correct," as well as to what is tidy, make this idea unacceptable. On some informal occasion an independent and imaginative hostess today might well find it amusing to ignore convention and use strewn flowers for a calculated effect of simplicity and for the conversation value of novelty and surprise. But how different is this approach, with its studied nonchalance and 20th-century desire for amusement and decorative value, from the medieval point of view in which strewn flowers were an established custom, providing the antiseptic protection of fragrance and the joy of symbolic connotation.

Almost all changes in table customs have motivations similarly keyed to the thought and temper of the time.

Le Grand d'Aussy, a late 18th-century historian of the manners and customs of the French people, writing about the medieval use of strewn flowers, expresses a typically 18th-century point of view with little understanding of the significance of flowers in the Middle Ages. He says, rather condescendingly, that people at that earlier time "had to employ whatever Nature offered to the eye," but this, he explains was "before Art had invented beautiful objects with which to adorn the table." It was inconceivable to him that anyone could have preferred humble flowers if the elaborate and exquisite ornaments of porcelain, silver, or silver gilt, the beguiling mechanical surprises, and other "fairy-like extravagances of magnificence and luxury" of the 18th century had been available. He does admit, however, that in the 17th century Louis XIV, well aware of the inventions of art and able to command any luxury his heart desired, was still fond of flowers and loved to have them on his table. The historian seems to consider this passion a charming eccentricity which could be indulged, even if it were not the fashion, by a great king who was a law unto himself.

It is both interesting and true that most references to flowers on the table in the 17th century (at least those that are available) relate to the court of Louis XIV. "Natural" flowers observed at many of the fetes given by, or in honor of, this king are frequently described in terms of astonishment both at the novelty of the idea and at the lavishness with which fresh flowers were displayed. Obviously the king's artists and masters of ceremonies saw the possibilities of exploiting this strange fancy of his as a novelty and took care to serve it up with appropriate extravagance. If flowers he must have, no humble violets or primroses would be scattered hit or miss on his table. They must be "rare and beautiful" and must be displayed in equally rare and beautiful containers.

Imagine a table fifty feet long and six and a half feet wide bearing "nineteen open-work baskets of silver or gilded copper" filled with anemones, hyacinths, Spanish jasmine, and orange blossoms, all in the dead of winter as they were in array at a January wedding in 1680 at Versailles. On this sumptuous table a garland of flowers, "also natural," bound one basket to the next. Sixteen candles illuminated each basket, adding to the brilliance of the baskets themselves "and the ribbons which ornamented them," the whole offering a "truly ravishing spectacle to the eye."[2]

Quantity combined with rarity! Novelty combined with extravagance! What could be more impressive to a court wanting and expecting to be impressed? Spring flowers in such profusion in January must have taxed even the resources of the King's greenhouses, then maintained chiefly for the cultivation of fruit, and of the famous Orangerie at Versailles which could, of course, have supplied orange blossoms.

It is probable that some of the flowers for such occasions actually came from Italy or Spain, carried carefully over the mountains in boxes which were made especially "for carrying flowers a long distance in winter" (Plate 43).

Jean Babelon, a modern writer on French *orfèvrerie,* gives an account of a supper given at Versailles in the 17th century in honor of Mme. de La Vallière describing a table ornamented with twenty-four grand silver pots filled with flowers. Winter or summer, when fresh flowers were used the accent was on quantity and lavish extravagance. On another occasion at Versailles "a strip of flowers" was used which went the length of the table and was changed with each course.[3] The flowers were probably bound into a garland to facilitate its removal and the placing of a fresh "strip."

Tiny shrubs, probably smartly clipped in the manner of garden topiary work, were a favorite form of decoration at the dessert. Once, it is reported, little potted shrubs were used, hung with preserved fruits and ribbon garlands.[4] At another gala, a vase of silver filigree held an orange tree covered with flowers and fruit. All around the base were "eight baskets and eight smaller vases, all sixteen filled with flowers."[5]

It is significant to note how often 17th- and 18th-century accounts are careful to differentiate between "natural" flowers and the artificial ones which were so much in fashion. According to Victor Gay's glossary of Medieval and Renaissance usage, artificial flowers had been made in France in the 15th century. In England they are mentioned in the accounts of the revels at court in the reigns of Queen Elizabeth I and King James I, for among stage properties and accessories purchased were such items as "one silk tree for a device in one of the candellsticke," some "lardge sylke fflowers," and "branches of flowers made of ffethers." But "new" artificial flowers from Italy, introduced into France in the 17th century, attempted to rival some very beautiful ones imported from China which, according to Diderot's *Encyclopédie,* "were made very perfectly but of a material very fragile when dry." No one was quite sure what this material might be. Some thought it the pith of some native tree; others, remembering the "crafty enchanters" of the East, suspected it was a secret composition known only to the Chinese. In any event it hardly seemed practical to import from such a distance anything so fragile and so expensive. Italian flowers made of silk, feathers, or cloth were more durable and apparently realistic enough to satisfy the 17th-century passion for being fooled, which, if it could be gratified, assured instant success to any host. This theater-loving society had a great fondness for make-believe. Any form of *trompe l'oeil* ("fools the eye") was sure to please.

By the 18th century artificial flowers were definitely the rage all over Europe. Especially notable were those made in Paris by one M. Seguin, a native of Mendes. He was a trained chemist and also a botanist whose superior knowledge of plants in all stages of bloom made his flowers surpass all others in realism. Uses for artificial flowers were many: to wear, to decorate interiors, or to display as objects of art or "curiosity." But Diderot, speaking of these exceptionally fine flowers says that they were used chiefly "in the Desserts," meaning to ornament the miniature gardens then fashionable for the table plateau on grand occasions.[6]

It is because of this great fashion for artificial flowers that there are so few references to the use of fresh ones in the 18th century. Indeed at this time real flowers were regarded as rather poor substitutes for those of porcelain or silk, particularly on the table. Hannah Glasse,[7] in *The Compleat Confectioner* (1762), says very firmly, "You must have artificial flowers of all sorts," then adds rather condescendingly, "and some natural out of a garden in summer do very well intermixed." However, enough mention is made of fresh flowers to prove that they were sometimes used casually in diverting and imaginative ways or, occasionally, even set forth on the plateau in elaborate, conversation-provoking containers.

Such an intricate contrivance was designed in 1770 by Louis XV's florist, de Lorme, considered "one of the most skilful decorators for the desserts," who constructed a glass tube to which were attached by metal rings many smaller tubes filled with flowers, arranged in a spiral around the central one. This gave the effect of a garlanded column which was fastened to a base and fitted with a capital, "the whole crowned with a magnificent basket of the most beautiful and most showy flowers."[8] This may have been similar to a metal column illustrated in Ferrari's *Flora* (Plate 44) which was to be used with very short-stemmed flowers so as "not to interfere with the design of the vase itself." Such elaborate devices are less to our liking today than the suggestion of Le Grand d'Aussy that "when the season permits" porcelain figures and little phials of glass filled with flowers could be attached with wax to the edge of a mirror plateau. Presumably, a porcelain temple or a pyramid of confectionery or fruit would be in the center.

By mid-18th century fresh flowers in winter, so rare in the 17th century, had become available to people of average wealth so it was not necessary to wait "until the season permitted" to enjoy them. There must have been plenty of people who preferred them despite the fashion for artificial flowers, because in December of 1765 "le Sieur Corby fils," a florist whose greenhouses were installed on the rue Roquette in Paris, announces in *L'Avant Coureur* that "in spite of the fact that one is in the midst of winter," he is able to offer "roses, pinks, hyacinths, liotripes and narcissus of Constantinople, all at a reasonable price."

Perhaps it was here that Talleyrand obtained the flowers for his luncheon in honor of the Turkish ambassador in 1797. La Marquise de La Tour du Pin was there and describes the party in her *Journal d'Une Femme de Cinquante Ans* as a spectacular affair with the buffet "half as high as the windows, garnished with exquisite dishes mingled with vases of the rarest flowers." Guests were not seated at table, she remarked, but at comfortable sofas about the room with small tables drawn up before them, not unlike a popular form of buffet luncheon today.[9]

Shortly after the turn of the century, in 1807, this same lady also tells of "a charming little surtout," or centerpiece, which she and her daughter constructed for a country wedding at her Chateau at Bouilh, the names of the bridal couple, "Henri and Eliza," written with flowers on a bed of moss.[10] Doubtless the moss rested upon a handsome silver or mirror plateau, an indispensable piece of table equipment as a base for any elegant centerpiece in the 18th or early 19th century.

Similar flat centerpieces with decorative patterns worked in flowers—a monogram, a coat of arms, or other device—were a late 18th-century fashion originating in Poland where short-stemmed flowers with no foliage were embedded in moss or wet clay, with a solid background of lesser flowers in a contrasting color. La Marquise de La Tour du Pin, a lady of discrimination and charm, may have done something attractive with this idea, but one shudders at the thought of such centerpieces made by the commercial "decorator for the desserts" who sometimes cared more for novelty than taste. Le Grand d'Aussy himself, who describes this Polish fashion, issues a warning that it is difficult to preserve all this covering of flowers from "a certain confusion, overpowering and fatiguing to the eye," and that flowers thus applied might lose the "elegant and gracious effect that is given by the light stem on which they are delicately poised."

A record of a more charming, artless way of using natural plant material is Mrs. Delany's enchanting description of a breakfast she was planning at her home in Delville, near Dublin, for a June morning in 1750. This talented artist, famous for her needlework, shell work, and marvelous flowers of cut paper, writes to her sister, Mrs. Dewes, that she has discovered a new breakfasting place "in the shade of nut trees . . . impenetrable to the sun's rays." She goes on to say that she has ordered cherries, strawberries, and nosegays to be laid on the table and has appointed a harper "to be here to play to us during the repast, who is to be hid among the trees." She also tells us, at the end of that same June, of breakfasting at her friend Mrs. Vesey's where the meal was served in the dairy "and the table *strewed with roses*." Her emphasis of this fact seems to imply that she considered this carrying "Gothick" taste just a bit too far.

A delightfully casual use of fresh flowers fashionable in the 18th century was as garnish for supper dishes, with nasturtiums in July and primroses, marguerites, and orange blossoms recommended for other seasons. Not a new idea by any means, as medieval dishes are described as "planted in 'violettes, primrosses,' or 'floures of borage,' and a certain dish of stewed apples" was to be "ornamented with 'floures of the same tre.' "[11]

The Renaissance, too, saw flowers used in this way. The great charger that Titian's daughter carries aloft is garnished with flowers and so is the dish of fruit borne by a handmaiden in Ghirlandaio's painting of the birth of St. John. Through the 16th and 17th centuries this tradition continued. Jan ("Velvet") Brueghel in "The Allegory of the Senses" decks a molded fruit jelly with a fresh carnation, and Zurbarán tops an enchanting basket of oranges with orange blossoms. Another painting by Zurbarán shows a porcelain bowl of pears, flaunting a fruited spray of their own tree, with roses, Ismene lilies, jasmine, and marigolds as well (Plate 45). No century seems to have neglected this custom, a charming survival of the medieval strewn flowers. Chardin, in the early 18th century, painted a flower-adorned cream puff and tucked flowers into the high pyramid of fruit (Plate 56). By the 19th century the fashion had evidently reached America, for Robert Roberts, butler at Governor Gore's mansion in Waltham, Massachusetts, wrote *A House Servant's Directory* (1828) advising that supper dishes "ought always to be garnished with green parsley and flowers as they give a supper table a most sublime appearance, and particularly in summer time when everything is green and in bloom."

In the 19th century, both in England and in America, flowers on the table are more frequently mentioned, but they are still often artificial and almost always subordinated to the fruits for the dessert instead of being featured in the center of the plateau. Hannah Glasse, an 18th-century authority on household management whose books still appeared in 19th-century editions, recommended for the dessert "bottles of flowers prettily intermixed" among the "jellies, creams . . . crisp'd almonds and little knicknacks." Beauvillier's *Art of French Cookery*, 1827 (an English edition of *L'Art du Cuisinier* by the same author, 1814), gives directions for ornamenting the plateau with "elegant trifles," such as "nests of moss with plovers' eggs, sugar plumbs, grapes or any other delicate fruits *en chemise* [dipped in white of egg, then in powdered sugar]," interspersed with "small moss baskets of roses, violets and other sweet smelling delicate flowers." He also offers the rather extraordinary suggestion of "herbaceous flowers *en chemise*."[12]

While the practice of dipping small fruits in white of egg and powdered sugar is attractive and well known, it may seem hardly adaptable to flowers, yet experiments with this dubious suggestion are both surprising and delightful. Flowers thus treated have the stiff, gleaming surface and high-lighted sparkle of porcelain and must have made a truly charming "ornament for the plateau" (Plate 37). One can see how, by reason of their resemblance to expensive porcelain flowers, they would then have been much admired. Dipping flowers in sugar was a revival of a much earlier custom. According to Lu Emily Pearson in *Elizabethans at Home* (Stanford, 1957), Sir Hugh Platt in the 16th century gives a recipe for preserving flowers in rose water and sugar. Sir Hugh specifies that it must be "the best refined sugar" and that "it must be hard and glitter like diamonds."

In contrast to the general trend of "moss baskets" and "little knicknacks" in the early 19th century, we do find an important flower arrangement in the center of the Austrian emperor's table in a water color of about 1826 (Plate 46). There is no plateau, and the vase is tall and slender with the tightly massed bouquet high above eye level. The arrangement is surmounted by an enormous Crown Imperial *(Fritillaria imperialis)* which seems to follow the 17th-century dictum expressed in Ferrari's *Flora* that "the most noble flower must be at the top."[13] But surely would this not have been considered very old fashioned in 1826? Nearly all early 19th-century authorities advise quite otherwise. In *Le Bouquet de Sentiment* (1816) by Mme. G. (evidently a lady of quality who wished to remain anonymous), a chapter on "The Manner of Grouping Flowers" tells us that the most beautiful and the largest flowers must be placed low and in the center, a precept more in line with present-day flower-show schools. Mme. G. seems to have been ahead of her time in other respects, as she explains the science of color harmony and advises that if yellow is the principal color in an arrangement, one must "be sure to introduce a little lavender or pale blue."[14]

The Austrian emperor's table, however, in spite of adhering to outmoded rules in the matter of arrangement, may have started a trend for larger and more important flower vases as centerpieces. When Madame Bovary, the socially ambitious heroine of Flaubert's mid-19th-century novel, went to dinner at the Marquis d'Andervillier's she was impressed by the elegance of it all. "The candles in the candelabra reflected long flames on the silver dish covers; the cut crystal, in the light steam, sent back pale rays; bouquets were placed in a line the whole length of the table."

Equally romantic, in this era, was the Victorian epergne, now provided with a trumpet-shaped vase at the top to hold flowers. There was also the "March" stand, arranged by the Misses March, which appeared in 1861, making a great sensation at a London flower show. This was a simplified version of the epergne in ordinary glass, not in itself an art object and intended to be almost completely hidden by the fruit or flowers. It consisted of two flat, shallow receptacles fastened at top and bottom to a tall slender glass rod (Plate 47). Flowers in the larger container at the base, impaled in sand or clay, were short stemmed. For the upper receptacle, flowers that drooped or trailed or had sentimental connotations were preferred. It was recommended by Mr. T. C. March in his book *Flower and Fruit Decoration,* London, 1862, that something should be induced to twine around the glass rod, such as "coboea, jessamine or passion flower."

Though the "March" stand carried its burden high above eye level and its slender supporting rod did not really prevent a view of the guests opposite, which had been one objection to the epergne, the next trend dispensed with any flowers that might interfere with the view across the table. Only candelabra and fruit compotes were allowed height. For the plateau, still fashionable and now equipped with zinc trays fitted inside its rim, short-stemmed flowers were arranged in moss or sand. Soon all containers were discarded, and flat, overlapping leaves were arranged directly on the cloth in wreaths and arabesques, much in the manner of Victorian garden design. John Perkins, in his 1877 book on *Floral Designs for the Table,* endorsed, and perhaps introduced, this method. His designs utilized sparse, interlocking curves or geometric patterns of "ornamental leaves and flowers elegantly combined" (Plate 48) which provided a garden-like setting for the "lamps" and fruit compotes which rose like fountains or statuary in their midst.

With the increasing affluence of the middle classes, however, this degree of restraint was soon considered rather parsimonious, and in the 1890's competitive extravagance brought back a lavish use of flowers. Floral centerpieces in Europe and America for several decades thereafter seemed to exist merely to exhibit an ostentatious and pretentious display of the most expensive, long-stemmed, "hot-house" flowers.

Sociably inclined diners often complained that they could not see the guests sitting across the table. It is said that Theodore Roosevelt, when in the White

House, detested the monstrosities of long-stemmed roses or carnations imbedded in a haze of asparagus fern created by florists. He always had these bouquets quietly removed before State dinners, muttering that when you went on a picnic you didn't sit around a *bush!*

Interest in flower arrangement, which became increasingly widespread in the 1920's and '30's, banished, we hope for all time, overcrowded and tasteless pincushions or towering barriers of flowers shrouded in gypsophila and fern. Their disappearance coincided with the disappearance of the parlor maid who had arranged them. Today we have learned to be more imaginative in our use of flowers, selecting them carefully for their special appropriateness to the general character and color harmony of the room and for their decorative quality in relation to everything on the table, including the food itself. But we should watch a tendency to be too finicky and "arty" in our efforts. All signs point to the need for a return to simpler massed arrangements, with the realization that it is possible to give a joyous sense of *flowers* and the reward of fragrance without creating a wall of fuzzy confusion in the center of the table.

*   *   *

Many and delightful are the descriptions of flowers used not on the table but nearby to add beauty and fragrance to the surroundings.

In Renaissance paintings flowers are often placed about a room where people are dining. Sometimes roses are caught up behind a painted coat of arms on the wall, or vases of flowers are placed on a high mantel or the projection of a cornice. In his "Last Supper" Ghirlandaio painted two lovely vases of flowers on a ledge high above the scene.

Louis XIV's suppers were frequently held in the garden at Versailles and natural floral settings were planned especially for important occasions. Mme. de Sévigné wrote to her daughter about a collation served "in a place carpeted with jonquils," and in another letter she spoke of the rumor that at a forthcoming gala at Chantilly there would be "a thousand crowns worth of daffodils alone . . . judge of the rest by that!" On one occasion in a *bosquet* in the garden at Versailles, "all the pilasters [of clipped evergreens] terminated in vases filled with flowers."

Flowers were always used in unique and ingenious ways at the court of this king. When a theatrical performance was held near a fountain in the great garden at Versailles it was feared that the noise of the water splashing in the pool might drown out the music of the violins and the voices of the performers. In addition to great vases of flowers at the edge of the pool, six porcelain vases filled with flowers were set in the basin of the fountain to muffle the sound as the water fell from six jets issuing from a *corne d'Amalthée* upheld by three little Tritons of bronze doré. Water was also intercepted by a great crown of flowers on the heads of the group of Tritons, for the same reason.[15]

With the coming of the 18th century, flowers continued to be used to decorate dining rooms. Vases were placed on brackets (Plate 49) or over doorways, and many garlands, now slender and delicate (and more likely than not, artificial), swung gaily from point to point.

Mrs. Philip Lybbe Powys, in her diary of 1777, admired a supper room "decorated with festoons of flowers in the most elegant taste," but she does not say whether they were artificial or real. On the table at the same party, however, she does mention "festoons and wreaths of artificial flowers, prettily disposed."

In England the Elizabethan custom of using flowers or foliage to ornament a fireplace in summer, often with strange combinations of herbs and even fruits growing "on a fine bank of moss," was still followed in the 18th century. But instead of banks of moss and growing plants, special vases called "bough pots" were made for cut flowers or shrub branches to carry on the tradition of "chimney flowers." This custom did not please John Byng (later Fifth Viscount Torrington), a crotchety English diarist of the 18th century who complained, when dining out on a chilly May evening, that "here were no fires but an elegant assortment of geraniums, and of myrtles, forced you to endeavour to hope that summer was coming." Today many an American traveling in England in summer would also prefer a cheery blaze on a damp evening to the bouquets or potted plants which so often inhabit fireplaces there.

The 18th-century fondness for wall vases may be judged by the number of existing examples seen in antique shops and museums today. This idea we should make use of far more often than we do, for with space so limited in our smaller houses and apartments, a wall vase has the advantage of placing flowers high enough to be seen yet well out of the way. A favorite form in the late 18th century when classic designs were in favor was the cornucopia, Greek symbol of fruitfulness and plenty (Plate 38), and good reproductions as well as originals of these are available today. We should be on the lookout for modern interpretations as well.

The idea of using flowering plants indoors in winter to give a party a festive air, greatly fostered by the Victorians who filled their conservatories, hallways, and bay windows with flowers and exotic plants of all kinds, continues to the present day. New interpretations of this idea found in ultramodern houses are built-in "planters" to take advantage of the light and warmth that modern window walls afford. In older houses any sunny window has its quota of house plants, and bay windows are often added to give more room for the enjoyment of flowering plants in winter.

In the 18th century the fashion of decorating a supper room with plants was prevalent throughout Europe. Christopher Marsden in *Palmyra of the North* (London, 1943) tells us that at the court of the Empress Anne of Russia in the early 1730's "even in the coldest weather the rooms were kept perfectly warm and decorated with orange trees and myrtles in full bloom, ranged in rows so as to form avenues on either side of the room, where company could 'sit out' only leaving space for the dancers in the middle. The effect of these warm, fragrant artificial groves, with nothing but ice and snow outside the streaming windows, was enchanting."[16] The gifted portrait painter Mme. Vigée-Lebrun, who visited Russia during her exile at the time of the French Revolution, also expressed her amazement at the Russians' use of fresh flowers in winter and at the warmth and comfort of palace interiors there. The rooms were "perfumed with warm vinegar into which were thrown branches of mint giving a very agreeable and wholesome odour."

The fashion for blossoming plants indoors in winter was not so easily followed in America in the 18th century. There were few greenhouses and in mid-19th century even a conservatory was considered an unusual feature. In the 1840's Mrs. James Rush, a famous Philadelphia hostess who never did things by halves, had two much-talked-of conservatories, one at either side of her ballroom, and her husband installed aviaries there, adding the magical surprise of bird song to the pleasure of flowers in winter. Mrs. Rush, it is said, paid the most minute attention to details when planning her balls and suppers, even to the "ribbons for the programmes and the oranges and lemons to be hung on the orange and lemon trees."[17]

Banks of hothouse flowers at an official party in Washington in the 1830's are described in the memoirs of Jessie Benton Fremont, daughter of Senator Thomas Benton of Missouri. She had been taken as a child to see the White House in readiness for a State occasion. "I have the beautiful recollection of the whole stately house adorned and ready for the company," she records, ". . . the great wood fires in every room, the immense number of wax lights softly burning, the stands of camellias and laurestinas banked row upon row, the glossy green leaves bringing into full relief their lovely waxlike flowers; after going

PLATE 37: Herbaceous flowers "en chemise"; recommended in an early 19th-century cookbook. The flowers first had to be dipped in white of egg and then rolled lightly in powdered sugar to give a hard, glistening surface resembling the fashionable porcelain flowers. (*Arrangement by the author; photograph by Francis Lambert*)

PLATE 38: Flowers nearby in a wall pocket. This wall vase of mid-18th-century salt-glaze stoneware is gay with nasturtiums arranged to continue the swirling line of the horn of plenty. *(Wall vase from collection of Nina Fletcher Little; arrangement by the author; photograph by George M. Cushing)*

PLATE 39: Detail of border of strewn flowers in a Flemish breviary, *c.* 1500. The flowers are drawn with loving precision and clearness. *(Mayer van der Bergh Museum, Belgium)*

PLATE 40: Detail of strewn flowers in altarpiece by Ludger Tom Ring the Younger; German, 1522–84. *(Metropolitan Museum of Art, New York; gift of J. Pierpont Morgan, 1917)*

PLATE 41: Sweetmeats with foliage and banners. Banners and a sprig of foliage ornament a dish of sweetmeats in "The Sense of Taste," by Jan ("Velvet") Brueghel, 1568–1625. Plate 122 shows another part of the painting of which this is a detail. *(Prado, Madrid)*

PLATE 42: "The Painter and His Wife," by the Master of Frankfurt, 15th century. On the table are simple field flowers casually thrust into a pottery jar. The pair enjoys a little fruit and wine. *(Courtesy, Baron van der Elst, Belgium)*

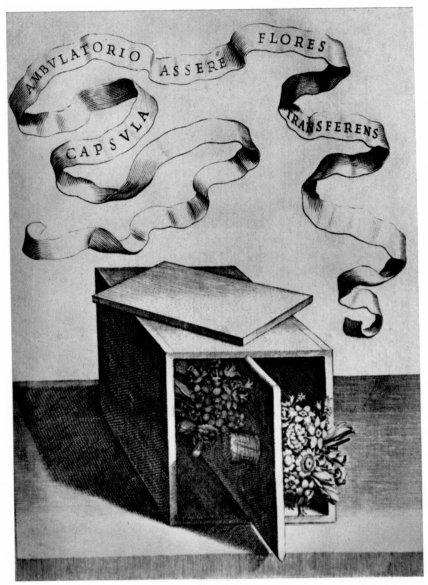

PLATE 43: An ingenious box for transporting flowers in winter, 1638. Bunches of flowers with their stems wrapped in moss were inserted in opposite directions in holes made in the central panel. This was then pushed back and the lid put on. The box could be fastened to the saddle bags and carried safely over the mountains in winter. *(From* Flora *by Ferrari; Rome, 1638)*

The Women's Pavilion at Saint Anthony's Hospital will be opening August 1. But before we open, we would like to give you a "sneak preview" of the newest addition to Saint Anthony's.

While at the Open House, you will have the chance to tour o... beautifully decorated birthing suites, nursery, operating roo... facilities and more. Plenty of...

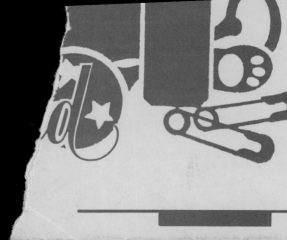

PLATE 44: A column for flowers, 17th century. This piece, "pierced through the entire body yet . . . not spill the water from any part," satisfied the delight in being fooled. This effect was achieved by the series of little cups attached to the long pole in the center which was concealed inside the column. Flower stems inserted in the holes in the outer vessel could reach water at any point. The vase on the left had an equally ingenious arrangement. The water was contained in several compartments and transmitted to the next by means of metal tubes. (From Flora by Ferrari; Rome, 1638)

PLATE 45: A bowl of pears. A Spanish still-life painting attributed to Francisco de Zurbarán, *c.* 1633–44, shows the fruit garnished with flowers. *(Art Institute of Chicago; Wirt D. Walker Fund)*

PLATE 46: The Austrian emperor's dining table. Note the elaborately folded napkins, a survival of a 17th-century fashion. *(Print Department, Metropolitan Museum of Art; from album of watercolors by Johan Stephan Decker offered in 1826 to the Princess Marie d'Orleans, daughter of King Louis Philippe)*

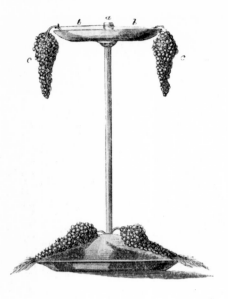

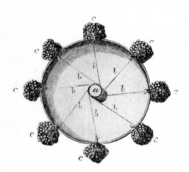

PLATE 47: Diagram of "March" stand in process of arrangement, showing how grapes are held in place (Figure 4 shows finished arrangements). *(From* Flower and Fruit Decoration *by T. C. March; London, 1862; courtesy Massachusetts Horticultural Society)*

PLATE 48: Design for table decoration in the garden-parterre manner. This design uses variegated geranium leaves overlapping one another and laid directly on the cloth. The leaves are of the variety known as Mrs. Polluck, the brightest leaves possible of uniform size being selected, thoroughly cleaned, and the leaf stalk cut completely off. No. 1 "may be an epergne filled with flowers, or a plant. Nos. 2 indicate glass tubes of cut flowers, Nos. 3 for fruit, Nos. 4 for dishes of roses." *(From* Floral Designs for the Table *by John Perkins; London, 1877; courtesy, Massachusetts Horticultural Society)*

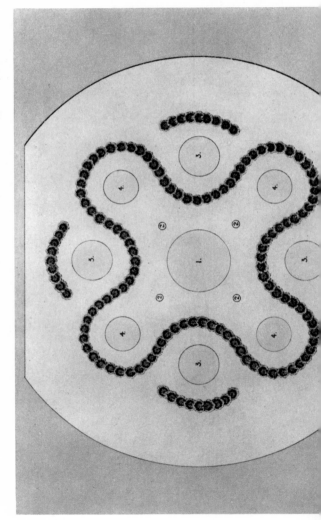

PLATE 49: Flower vase on high bracket at a Venetian carnival. Color and fragrance are thus supplied to the guests seated at a small table in a gaily garlanded pavilion (also see Plate 32). *(Detail from "The Carnival in Venice," by Rudolph Byss; c. 1707; courtesy, Wadsworth Athenaeum, Hartford)*

PLATE 50: French gilt-bronze fruit dish. This piece is part of the Monroe centerpiece ordered by President Monroe in 1817. *(White House Historical Association; photograph by National Museum of Decorative Art)*

all through the silent waiting fairyland we were taken to the State dining room where was the gorgeous supper table shaped like a horseshoe and covered with every good and glittering thing French skill could devise, and at either end was a monster salmon in waves of meat jelly."[18] What a picture this evokes of a White House party in an age of elegance, one that we can visualize against a background of early Empire classicism, as the house was restored after the fire of 1814 in this French style which was then at the height of fashion.

With succeeding administrations, alas, the White House fell prey to late Victorian "persuasions of fashion," and the camellias and laurestinas "banked" on State occasions gave way to aspidistras and potted palms to be admired against the "steamboat palace decor" which was inflicted upon the White House in the Grant administration. Fashions in table decoration followed the same lugubrious pattern, although in 1861 Mrs. Lincoln, according to the *New York Star* (quoted by Irving Stone in his biography of Mrs. Lincoln, *Love Is Eternal*), is credited with the good taste of using fresh flowers from the White House conservatories and grounds instead of the stiff artificial bouquets favored on the table in preceding administrations.

In the 1880's a fashion was introduced in Washington perhaps inspired by John Perkins' *Floral Designs for the Table*. At a dinner honoring President and Mrs. Cleveland, according to an undated Washington newspaper clipping, "the flower of thought," known to be Mrs. Cleveland's favorite, was chosen. A centerpiece and two end pieces of yellow and purple pansies were arranged in flat "oval cushions," with pansies "strewn on the cloth" between.

President Grant's dinner tables were far less restrained, "loaded with mountains of flowers and trailing vines and ribbons,"[19] which led to a still more deplorable fashion described by Ellen Maury Slaydon, wife of a Texas Congressman. In her journal (recently published as *Washington Wife*) she describes a fashionable luncheon table in 1898 which she found "too much beribboned" for her taste, as "ribbons and gravy are so incompatible." She was also not impressed by "broad satin stripes running diagonally across with big bows, like a little girl's sash, at each corner."

After the turn of the century Theodore Roosevelt's moose heads looked down incongruously from the walls of the State dining room upon massive floral creations submerged in fern, and taste remained at a low ebb during the first decades of the 20th century. A hopeful sign of the return of real distinction on a White House table was shown by President and Mrs. Truman at their dinner honoring Queen Elizabeth II of Great Britain when, as a princess, she and

Prince Philip visited Washington in 1951. On that occasion the handsome French Empire centerpiece of gilt bronze, purchased for the White House by President Monroe in 1817, was brought out from long forgotten storage to grace the table in the newly renovated State dining room.

Perhaps the report of this hidden treasure in the White House store rooms was one of the many factors that inspired Mrs. John F. Kennedy, soon after her husband's inauguration, to restore the whole house to "its full historical significance," bringing back "the old and beautiful things which symbolize the dignity of the President's House," and, by the creation of a permanent White House Historical Association, providing it with a measure of protection from whatever vagaries of fashion may descend upon Washington in the future. The success of this immense and difficult undertaking, so imaginatively conceived and so thoughtfully carried out, is now part of the history of the house itself, and Mrs. Kennedy has left the mark of her own elegance upon it.

The White House, "adorned and ready for the company," today must indeed satisfy a child's idea of fairyland. Especially so fulfilling is the State dining room, all white, gold, and sparkling crystal, with the lovely Monroe center-piece on its ornamental plateau, its gilded nymphs balancing gilt baskets of fruit or flowers on their heads (Plate 50). The note of gold is repeated with lustrous vermeil (silver-gilt) accessories and softly burning candles in gilded candelabra and chandeliers.

As for adults, in this era of make-shift and practicality in the domestic arts, the aura of dignity and perfection of this lovely table may well remind us that these qualities are not unattainable in our own lives, a part of our heritage as the White House itself now demonstrates. Let the experience of it not only be a "beautiful recollection" but a lasting influence on all who are privileged to see "the gorgeous supper table" in readiness for a State occasion.

❧ FIVE

Appeal of the Pyramid

How to make a fine pyramid of fruit was the concern of every European head steward or major-domo from the Middle Ages well into the 19th century. There were, of course, various changing fashions in the height and breadth and in methods and devices for constructing these towering centerpieces, but always the same general form prevailed. This was not only because piling up fruit in this fashion was a natural and logical way of getting enough on a plate but also because the form itself was an impressive method of presentation.

There is something undeniably noble and majestic about a pyramid, *any* pyramid! This is partly through association, for we do think at once of the solitary grandeur of the Egyptian pyramids and of the slender but still pyramidal soaring of a church spire. The Oriental pagoda with its basically pyramidal form also conveys the same idea of impressive height and noble aspiration. But aside from such associations, there is a purely optical power of suggestion inherent in the form itself. A sense of strength comes from its symmetrical solidity, which also lends unity to the design, and the climax of its pointed top seems to lead the eye upward as if a deferential offering were being held aloft.

Marco Polo, during his travels in China in the 13th century, was struck with "an impression of wealth and splendor" when he saw the great "Mount" in the garden of Kublai Khan at Kambalu, its cone-shaped hill planted with rare trees and crowned with a tall, pyramidal pagoda, and he may have been similarly impressed by the Oriental custom of piling fruit into high pyramids as table decoration. Since a 12th-century Chinese painting on silk (Plate 53) shows handsome pyramids on the table at the garden repast of a literary gathering, they must surely have been used in the 13th century at the court of the great Khan. In fact this form was still a favorite with the Chinese as late as the 17th century.

In the East traditional ways with plant material change very little from one century to another, and even today natives of Bali, Korea, Thailand, and other countries of Asia and Asia Minor make fantastically high pyramids of fruit or flowers on ceremonial occasions. Naturally this dramatic idea, if brought back to Venice by Marco Polo, would have appealed to European kings, princes, or aspiring nobles eager to give an impression of their own wealth and splendor, and fine pyramids of fruit on their tables may have seemed one way of attaining this desired end.

Marco Polo's reports of the luxury and magnificence of Eastern potentates were, at the time of his return to Venice, considered too chimerical to be believed, and medieval fruit pyramids, if they were based upon his descriptions, were only a timid echo of Oriental grandeur. Subsequent travelers to the Far East confirmed his statements, however, and by the 17th century, not to be outdone in matters of magnificence, head stewards at the court of Louis XIV in France vied with one another to construct fruit pyramids of ever more and more astonishing altitude (Plate 54).[1] To make them still more spectacular, they were built up on dishes of Oriental porcelain, then so rare and expensive in Europe that few could afford such luxury. Dishes were used in diminishing sizes with a layer of fruit between one dish and the next, making a pyramid which often reached to a height of three or four feet.

Needless to say such exaggerated displays presented a problem when they were carried in by a procession of lackeys at the dessert (Plate 55). Mme. de Sévigné, in an amusing letter to her daughter on Aug. 5, 1671, gives a deliciously satirical description of one such pyramid "of twenty porcelains" which came to grief at the very doorway with such a great clatter of falling fruit and crashing porcelain that it completely drowned out the music of the violins, the *hautbois,* and the trumpets. She remarked that doorways would now have to be made higher to admit such absurdities, "for our fathers did not forsee this sort of machine, since even they never dreamed that a door would have to accommodate anything higher than themselves." As for the objection that such pyramids, when they did reach the table without mishap, obscured one's view of the guests opposite, she observed dryly that the circumstance had its advantage as, "far from being offended . . . one is often glad, on the contrary, not to be able to see what they hide."

De La Quintinye, 17th-century agriculturist and orchardist to Louis XIV, also mocked these great "edifices" of fruit which were not eaten but were solely for decoration (Plate 56). Though admitting that they were "something rather grand and magnificent," he felt that "since it was the custom never to touch them they only did honor to the officer who had the patience to arrange them with such symmetry." He conceded that one "grand pyramid" might be kept undisturbed for the center of the table but begged that at least one pretty basket might be added in which the guests might find fruit to eat.[2]

Whenever a fashion reaches the point of ridicule, it is inevitably doomed. Whether it was the result of the triumph of Reason over Absurdity or that the ponderous magnificence of the Louis XIV style was on the wane, the "grand pyramids" of fruit went out of fashion and the 18th century, with its preference for elegance over bombast, found a more graceful as well as a more stable way of arranging the fruits for dessert.

In France and elsewhere on the Continent, this was accomplished by the *assiette montée,* sometimes called a *girandole* or an *assiette étagère,* a two-, three-, or four-tiered fruit stand of porcelain, silver, silver gilt, or glass. This stand held the fruits aloft in a distinguished manner with a delicacy and charm to match that of the other exquisite table appointments of the period. Confectioners in the late 18th century even furnished similar stands of gilded and embossed cardboard on which to display their candied fruits and cakes. These cardboard stands were beautifully made and were often ornamented with crystal prisms or porcelain figures and medallions.

In England, also, these appeared, but the idea of a decorative dessert stand was further developed there into the epergne, a Georgian invention which, despite its seemingly French name, was never referred to by that name in France (Chapter 6).

It is interesting that in both the *assiette montée* and the epergne the general pyramidal form was still maintained and that an effect of symmetrical, tapering height and solid grandeur was achieved in an elegant and sophisticated manner perfectly in accord with the taste of the 18th century. Both devices, with variations, continued to be fashionable through the 19th century. Their original ornamentation of rococo motifs or chinoiserie gave way to classic interpretations as that style began to dominate the scene, followed by Victorian versions in the romantic taste of the late 19th century.

All these "inventions of art" made it easy to achieve a pyramidal form, but there were still occasions for fruit pyramids on a flat surface, and the early 19th-century cookbooks show how this can be accomplished by the use of finely sifted and slightly dampened moss. Bernardi, an early 19th-century authority on the elegant presentation of the dessert, gives directions for making a pyramid of apples on such a container, as follows: "When you have dried them carefully with a linen cloth place a bed of moss on a plate; then place the fruits on top in a circle, with a little moss between each apple. Fill the middle with moss, then again make a bed of moss under the apples. Place the next row of apples again upon it, always putting a wisp of moss between each fruit and continue thus until a pyramid is formed. [Plate 51 shows contemporary pyramid of fruit according to these instructions.] Then place this plate on a basket of porcelain and put it on the table."[3]

This method of constructing a pyramid of fruit had probably been in use for some time. In fact one wonders if it must not have been the means of giving some stability to those towering fruit pyramids of the 17th century, as spagnum moss was then available and would have been a likely choice for this purpose. "Moss baskets" of both fruit and flowers are often mentioned, and in 17th- and 18th-century still-life paintings the use of moss as a foundation for both fruit and flowers can frequently be detected.

As for placing a plate with a fruit pyramid "on a basket of porcelain," this custom is explained in detail in *The Court and Country Cook* as early as 1702. Baskets, whether of wicker or porcelain, were fitted with thin wooden lids which rested on the inner ledge around the top. On this lid, to be covered with decorative paper of some kind (marbleized or tortoise-shell patterns were much admired), the plate was placed. Sometimes two plates could be accommodated on the lid of an oval basket, and borders of flowers or foliage were tucked in around the basket's edge. When no baskets were available, one could use "certain Tin Molds of the same shape," or small wooden stands on legs might answer. The illustration in Plate 57 shows baskets with pyramids of fruit or little cakes thus arranged on a hexagonal wooden stand known as a "Level," and the whole complex, with its lesser pyramids, itself takes an impressive pyramidal form (Plate 76).

All through the 18th and early 19th centuries we continue to find descriptions of "fruit elegantly elevated into pyramids," but later in the 19th century the conception of elegance, on the table at least, grew more and more restrained until it became almost niggardly.

Mme. Bovary aped her betters by arranging "pyramids of green-gages on vine leaves," though her mother-in-law thought she was being "too fine for her position." But Mme. Bovary had had a glimpse of the *haut monde* and knew that the old-fashioned abundance of an 18th-century dessert was scorned in the 19th century's best circles. Jane and Thomas Carlyle, who dined with Charles Dickens and his wife in 1849, were also aware of this change in fashion. Jane sniffed at Mrs. Dickens' "vulgar, overloaded" dessert with its quantities of artificial flowers, pyramids of figs, raisins, oranges, and whatnot, but, on the other hand, greatly admired the dessert at another dinner where the table was graced with "just four cowslips in china pots, four silver shells containing sweets and a silver filagree temple in the middle."[4]

Pyramids were not by any means out of fashion, but they lacked the opulent profusion so much favored in the 18th-century epergne. Instead small fruits like cherries and strawberries were piled up like cannon balls on low, footed salvers called *tazze* or on "vine leaves," and "mere thimblefuls of sweetmeats" were ranged on the mid-19th-century mirror plateau, tapering to an elegant point. They had a finicky air of overrefinement, like crooking the little finger that holds the tea cup. At the end of the century, when these pyramids could be refined no further, they faded away, like the old soldier, and eventually disappeared.

They were replaced for awhile by nondescript bowls of fruit which lacked the distinction of a fruit pyramid on a flat surface but certainly were much easier to arrange—too easy, perhaps, for those of us exhibiting in early 20th-century flower shows who needed more scope for our talents. In the 1930's, already fascinated with asymmetrical flower arrangements, we began to make our fruit arrangements asymmetrical as well, captivated by the possibilities for variety, for sweeping S-curves and decorative contrasts of form and color. We have been more or less preoccupied with them ever since.

Strange how we can become enamored of an idea, thinking it capable of endless interpretations, and then suddenly discover that we have wrung it dry! Now across our jaded vision comes the stunning pyramid of fruit, so long ignored, its handsome solidity and direct simplicity so appropriate in a modern setting that we find it in the very forefront of fashion. It has "high style" and is so "right" for the present moment (Plate 52).

It is also more practical for use at home, which may in part account for its revival. The flower-show method of constructing asymmetrical arrangements of fruit often involves impaling the fruit on needle holders or wired pegs which causes it to spoil rapidly and makes such arrangements suitable only for a one-day show or for a single important occasion. For everyday use we might condemn these "edifices" with de La Quintinye's objection that they only do honor to the one who has had the patience to arrange them, whereas a simple pyramid of apples in a copper dish or on a china compote would not only look very "smart" but would have the added advantage that if someone wanted to eat an apple he could just take one, without ruining Mother's Day.

For formal occasions or for the show, those longing for vanished elegance and for something a little more impressive may turn to the *assiette montée* or the epergne, using them in modern as well as traditional interpretations.

*   *   *

Pyramids of flowers, which have been intermittently fashionable through the centuries, may well have originated in the East. Alternated with the fruit pyramids on the 12th-century Chinese table mentioned above, there are small, neat pyramids of little white starry flowers in identical vases. This, owing to our study of Japanese flower arrangement, comes to us as a surprise for we have become accustomed to thinking of Oriental arrangements as asymmetrical. But we must realize that the Japanese style we know so well is but a late aspect of Eastern traditions. In Japan, as well as China in the 12th century, symmetry was observed not only at banquets but also in temple offerings, and this orderly and unexpectedly urbane table setting shows a sophistication in Oriental cultural life far beyond that of Europe in the same century.

In Indian miniatures representing festive scenes, pyramids of flowers often adorn even an informal garden repast, sometimes in little bottles ranged in a row around the edge of a carpet spread for an important personage and sometimes on a low stand with fruit (Plate 58). The regard for the pyramid is also demonstrated in the exaggeratedly high flower forms still followed in Thailand today. Sometimes these are similar to the high spiraling arrangements seen in Byzantine mosaics and sometimes are lower and more solid pyramids intricately patterned with flowers of contrasting colors and with a broken silhouette suggesting the pointed towers of a Siamese temple.

Wanting very much to make some of these dramatic pyramids as decorations for a reception at the opening of the "Arts of Thailand" show at the Boston Museum of Fine Arts in March of 1961, we asked a Thai student how they were done, but she could only say that they were made with wet sawdust and that it was "very difficult." It would be with wet sawdust! But we settled for today's plastic foam as a substitute, and while it was still difficult to get the

PLATE 51: A pyramid of plums in an early 19th-century setting; the family dining room of the Governor Gore mansion, Waltham, Massachusetts. The Canton china compote is raised on a Lazy Susan that belonged to Governor Gore, and the flowers, in Canton syllabub cups encircling the centerpiece. Little vases are often shown thus in contemporary engravings. The fruit pyramid is made according to Bernardi's directions, 1844. (*Arrangement by the author; photograph by Zitso Studio*)

PLATE 52: Today's cocktail buffet. Part of a buffet suggested by 17th-century still-life paintings. There are cocktail tomatoes in pyramids, an out-sized martini bottle, and a Victorian ink well (*Arrangement by the author; photograph by Zitso Studio*)

PLATE 53: Pyramids of fruit and flowers on Chinese table; detail from a 12th-century painting on silk. *(Chinese National Palace and Central Museums, Taiwan)*

PLATE 54: Buffet with high pyramids of fruit. Here is a buffet around the central fountain in the Cour de Marbre, Versailles. (see Plate 129) *(Detail of an engraving by Lepautre from* Les Divertissemens de Versailles *by André Félibien; Paris, 1676; courtesy, Harvard College Library)*

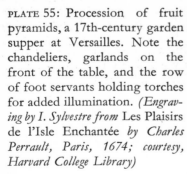

PLATE 55: Procession of fruit pyramids, a 17th-century garden supper at Versailles. Note the chandeliers, garlands on the front of the table, and the row of foot servants holding torches for added illumination. *(Engraving by I. Sylvestre from* Les Plaisirs de l'Isle Enchantée *by Charles Perrault, Paris, 1674; courtesy, Harvard College Library)*

PLATE 56: "Le Buffet," by Chardin; early 18th century. The painting
shows a pyramid of fruit garnished with flowers on a high wooden or
metal stand set inside a huge shallow porcelain charger. This pyramid is
reminiscent of the 17th century. *(Courtesy, National Museum of France)*

PLATE 57: Dessert "dressed upon a Level." (The Court and Country Cook, *1702; courtesy, Harvard College Library*)

PLATE 58: East Indian pyramid of flowers with fruit in a 17th-century Indian miniature. Although the vase is small, the stand with fruit accommodates the balance neatly. Note the details of carafe and wine glasses and the three fruits on an oblong dish at the top. (*From a portfolio of Indian miniatures in a series called* "Museum of Masterpieces"; *Les Éditions du Chêne, Paris*)

PLATE 59: "The Cloister School."
Here, nuns make pyramidal flower arrangements in the Byzantine style in 17th-century Italy. Similar arrangements were used on the table at the same period. *(Detail from a painting by Allesandro Magnasco; courtesy, Wadsworth Athenaeum, Hartford)*

PLATE 60: Baskets of flowers in pyramidal mounds on a rococo plateau. Hedges of sugar divide the sections of this garden parterre. (see illustration of this entire plateau in Plate 84) *(Detail from* Le Cannameliste Français, *1751; courtesy, Harvard College Library)*

PLATE 61: Table of Maria Theresa. Flower Pyramids in ornamental temples appear to be on the table during the main part of the meal, as the meat is about to be carved. *(Engraving from Austrian fete book, 1740; courtesy, Harvard College Library)*

PLATE 62: Rococo pyramid of sugar arabesques ornamented with sugar flowers. *(From* Le Cannameliste Français, *1751; courtesy, Harvard College Library)*

PLATE 63: Pyramidal container of painted tole. Moon moth pansies and white lilac buds with foliage of Euonymus vegetus are used; allowing the red tole container to show. (*Arrangement by the author; photograph by George M. Cushing*)

PLATE 64: Silver fruit stand. This piece is part of the surtout-de-table made by Christofle in 1853 for Napoleon III. The stand appears with a pyramid of fruit and flowers as exhibited at the Musée des Arts Décoratifs, Paris, in August, 1964. *(Courtesy, Christofle, Paris)*

PLATE 65: Pyramid of fruit and flowers suggested by early Siamese designs. *(Arrangement made by the author for a lecture at the Museum of Fine Arts, Boston; photograph by the museum)*

PLATE 66: Meissen vase of porcelain flowers, 18th century. Grouped in a tight low pyramid, flowers create the effect of a pointed lid to the vase. It is probable that real flowers, when used, were also arranged in this way in the 18th century. *(Early Meissen vase of porcelain flowers from the collection of Delia Spencer Field; courtesy of Catherine Beveridge; photograph by George M. Cushing)*

desired height and our spiral patterns were not as perfect as we would have wished, our pyramids seemed in character with the fantastic stupas of Siam. When we asked our little Thai friend what flowers were used, both her English and horticultural knowledge were woefully inadequate. All we could gather was that they were "like dry." March was no time to find much variety in dried material, but fortunately yellow and purple statice were available and these we used, punctuating our designs with pink gladiolus buds which, if not authentic, made exciting accents. Pyramids of fruit garnished with flowers also had an exotic Oriental effect (Plate 65).

* * *

The pyramid of flowers does not seem to have reached Europe until the early 17th century when flower arrangements are quite definitely pyramidal, solidly and symmetrically made, coming to a point at the top. Possibly these were introduced because of increasing contact with the East when Oriental pyramids of flowers could have been observed by many travelers. European church flowers followed Byzantine designs at this time (Plate 59), and even in the late 17th century, when flower paintings show chiefly S-curve, asymmetrical arrangements, those used on the table are still stiffly pyramidal, as table fashions usually lag a little behind fashions in general.

On 18th-century tables flower pyramids, as seen in the few pictorial records available, are usually low and elliptical in small oval baskets as in Roman or Byzantine mosaics, but one rococo centerpiece shown in *Le Cannameliste Fran-çais* has its baskets filled with high rounded pyramids (Plate 60). In an engraving of Maria Theresa at table, there are higher pyramids of flowers sheltered by ornamental temples of porcelain or silver gilt (Plate 61). That flower pyramids may have been even more sharply pointed at this time may be judged by some vases of porcelain flowers in which the blossoms take the form of a small narrow pyramid, closely set and almost suggesting a pointed lid to the vase (Plate 66). In a vase which is itself flower decorated, this close-set grouping helps to focus the eye on the flower arrangement and thus avoids the confusion of two conflicting patterns, an idea to be remembered when dealing with an ornately figured container.

Much higher pyramids of flowers were in fashion in the early 19th century, so much so that special, many-tiered vases were designed and sold to facilitate their construction. These vases of four or five compartments set a little distance apart on a central pole were extremely tall, narrowing toward the top, and were usually of painted tole. Metal handles, on the lowest compartment, were apt to be rings emerging from lions' mouths or rams' heads, and the vase stood on ball or claw feet. We see these containers occasionally in antique shops today, and interior decorators offer handsome reproductions of them (Plate 63), at a handsome price, as fruit and flower pyramids are momentarily high fashion.

It is probable that containers like these were used when James Smith Colburn, a Boston merchant, was entertained at dinner in Paris in 1801 by Necker, the celebrated French banker. Mr. Colburn was impressed by the table decoration on this occasion which consisted of "a large and elegant plateau with pyramids of all kinds of flowers, the most beautiful and costly, and all kinds of bottles of perfumes." The flowers, he adds, were "so elevated we could not see those on the other side of the table."[5]

During the Napoleonic period when the Empire style prevailed in France and was widely adopted elsewhere, the fondness for the grandiose undoubtedly allowed only the bottom compartment of these tall containers to show, the upper ones hidden by a solid pyramid of flowers. But today, unless required to be authentic at a flower show, one might take liberties, making the flowers spiral to the top and permitting glimpses of the colorful tole in between. A pair of these would be stunning on a buffet table or on pedestals at an afternoon reception, but not on a table where guests are seated, for, in spite of Mme. de Sévigné's reservations, we still prefer to see the guests opposite.

How long today's fashion for pyramids of fruit or flowers will last is problematical. At the moment it is "in" and we enjoy experimenting with it and adapting it to our needs. Even when, as a fad, we may be tired of it, we can still remember its possibilities whenever a special occasion or a special background seems to call for something rather lofty and magnificent. Symmetry and the pyramidal form set a fine mood of "consequence," and the past offers inspiration in great variety.

SIX

The Surtout & the Epergne

MUCH KUDOS can be achieved in any century, apparently, by the possession of an imposing centerpiece for the dinner table, beginning with a fantastic
wine fountain of silver or silver gilt on a grand table in the Middle Ages and
ending with an antique Georgian silver epergne, a superb piece of Steuben
glass, or any comparably fine and expensive ornament that today's hostess
might display with pride. The French, who have always had a special predilection for things of this kind and who have devised many variations of the centerpiece idea (with a different and strikingly appropriate name for each version),
set the fashion for the rest of Europe and inspired competition among goldsmiths everywhere to produce finer and more magnificent centerpieces according to every changing dictate of taste.

The origin of this type of decoration may well have been the nef, that
strange, glorified condiment stand in ship form (Plate 67) which appeared on
royal tables in medieval France, surrounded with mystery and symbolism both
secular and religious. Intricately wrought of precious metals and embellished
with jewels or colored enamel, this revered object, sometimes presented as a
votive offering to the church, was, when used on the table, the sovereign
prerogative of kings or members of the royal family.[1] It therefore had to be
admired from afar, but lesser nobles quite naturally yearned for their own status
symbols and craftsmen were quick to provide them, taking care to invent new
shapes and different functions so as not to encroach upon royal preserves.

131

The king's nef was useful as well as symbolic and ornamental. It held salt and rare spices for his needs, plus his personal eating utensils and certain bizarre objects such as a "serpent's tooth" or a "unicorn's horn,"[2] believed to have the power of detecting poison. But the table ornaments made for the lesser nobility, and frequently employed by royalty as well, were not at first used in this way. Massive and highly decorative, displaying fine workmanship and lavish use of rich materials, they served to promote admiring conversation between courses. They sometimes even took the form of wine fountains or other mechanical surprises to further enliven the tiresome interval during the change of service. For this reason they were called "entremets," or "between-dishes," a word also applied to other forms of entertainment that might be offered between courses.

During the Renaissance the less colorful word *milieu,* or "center," was given to this object, indicating that it had become more of a routine feature than a conversation piece. In the 17th century, when superlatives were the order of the day, the term *surtout-de-table,* often abbreviated to *surtout* as it is in France today, came into use to denote a splendid centerpiece, one that, as the word implies, was "above everything" on the table, not only in height but in the matter of importance and extent (Plate 68).

By this time the nef had lost its early mystic significance and, if it appeared at all, was merely a valuable antique ornament on the buffet, along with other inherited treasures such as the "gold cup enriched with sapphires" which appeared in the 1359 Inventory of King Charles V with the notation that it had belonged to Charlemagne. So much were antiques venerated in the 16th century that at a fete given at Fontainebleau by Francis I, celebrating the birth of the Princess Elizabeth, a pyramidal buffet held an immense quantity of the king's treasures, and "an officer stood by to give the history of each piece."[3] Many a nef from former days must surely have figured in this display.

By the 17th century, the *surtout* was the most important thing on the grand table and was a useful and handsome piece of equipment holding necessary condiments and adding side dishes for preserved fruits, and branches for candles. Though no longer restricted to royalty and not, like the nef in ship form, the *surtout* was a very grand affair indeed. Often pyramidal, it conveyed the impression of magnificence so desirable in the 17th century, and it appears to be the French counterpart of the "great standing salt," an imposing silver object which served a like purpose on the grand table in England at the same period.

The first mention to be found of the term *surtout* is in 1603 when Rosny, later the Duc de Sully, came as French ambassador to the court of James I, where he dined in State with the king at Greenwich on June 29th of that year. In his memoirs Rosny observes that on this occasion "a *Surtout* in the form of a pyramid containing the most costly vessels, and even enriched with precious stones" was placed in the middle of the table.

Later in the 17th century Louis XIV is also reported to have had a *surtout* which he used "when traveling in the country." Even when on a military campaign everything for a king's use had to be duly sumptuous, and this *surtout* no doubt was fully as grand as that of the English king. Nonetheless, Dangeau, who mentions it in his *Journal* of 1694, seems to have admired it chiefly because it was a new and efficient way of carrying the king's mealtime necessities in a compact and easily portable form. His entire dinner could be served in it and set before him with all accessories if he wished to dine, as he so often preferred to do, in a small remote country house without the annoyance of crowds or ceremony.

Louis XIV also had another splendid *surtout* on his table at Marly, this one of silver gilt, made on an ornamental base with eight branches for candles, four sugar boxes, casters for salt and pepper, and eight "children."[4] The latter may have been figures of boys or cupids incorporated in the base as if supporting the candles or side dishes, a typically baroque device, or perhaps they were free-standing to carry garlands from one to another as an extension of the center-piece at either end. Other *surtouts* of this period are reported to have had candle brackets and side dishes that were interchangeable, depending upon whether or not lights were needed, and some were even fitted with baskets for fruit or flowers.

One would expect this new type of centerpiece, which so delightfully com-bined usefulness and beauty with a heady dash of extravagance, to have had an instant success in a magnificent and luxury-loving court. But the development of the *surtout* was delayed and hampered during the 17th century, and in fact through the end of Louis XIV's reign (1715), by frequent royal edicts forbidding the use of silver for numerous domestic luxuries whenever the king needed money to pay for his overwhelming military disasters. Not only was the pro-duction of new silver table ornaments periodically halted but existing pieces were ordered melted down so that almost no examples of this period, alas, remain.

We read of one fascinating *surtout*, however, which was strangely prophetic of a new trend to be developed in England later on. It appeared in 1688 at a fete given by the Prince de Condé in honor of the Dauphin and was described by

Le Grand d'Aussy: "In the middle of a round table was elevated a great silver basket filled with fruit and flowers and supported by twelve openwork consoles. Each one of these consoles carried, on the outside, two little silver baskets of fruit . . . and connecting them all were garlands of flowers."[5]

This exuberant centerpiece certainly sounds like the forerunner of the English epergne and had, perhaps, been seen and copied by some of the French Huguenot silversmiths who fled to England at about this time to escape religious persecution. But if this interesting idea did come from France, the English did not adopt the French term, *surtout*. They called it an epergne. Since the word sounds like a French one but is not, this is a circumstance which has occasioned much speculation by those interested in the history of table ornaments.

It is generally agreed that the word "epergne" is an English corruption of the French word *épargne,* meaning "a saving or a treasury," but why the word was used in England and never in France to denote this type of centerpiece has not been satisfactorily explained. Writers on old silver appear to endorse the theory that, since fruit and sweetmeats (and sometimes, oddly enough, pickles or sea food!) were piled in one centerpiece in a great pyramidal complex of central basket and smaller swinging baskets hung from side brackets, guests could reach out and help themselves, and thus a saving of service was achieved. But this hardly seems logical. Whoever worried about saving service in the 18th century!

Another conjecture is that the shape of the little prongs from which the side baskets hang is similar to the long curved spout of a tall pitcher known as a "ewer." This piece stood on the buffet in the Middle Ages and was brought around, with its accompanying basin, so that guests could wash their hands, a ceremony which took place several times during a banquet at that time. It is noted that in French Canada this type of ewer is today referred to as an *épargne,* though the word is not now used in that sense in France.

It seems odd that no one has considered the importance of the secondary meaning of the word, "a treasury," which was in the 18th century its principal meaning. At that time the royal treasure was known as *l'Épargne.* Is it not reasonable to suppose that the epergne (or the *épargne,* as the English have been known to spell it both ways) was actually the place where all the fruits which were too rare or too beautiful to eat were *treasured* for the enjoyment of their decorative value alone! And is it not likely that the French silversmiths in England who may have brought with them the idea may also have chosen the name *épargne,* or treasury, which was soon corrupted into epergne?

As for the thought of guests reaching out and helping themselves to fruit displayed in the centerpiece, we have proof that this was considered the height of bad manners, as it certainly would be today. Both Rousseau and Voltaire, who notoriously scoffed at what seemed to them foolish conventions of society, committed this breach of etiquette and were gently but firmly scolded for it. At one dinner party Rousseau is said to have helped himself to a handsome peach at the very bottom of a fine pyramid of fruit thereby, of course, demolishing the whole towering work of art in the center of the table. His tactful hostess said sadly, "Rousseau, that is what you always do with all our systems; you pull down with a single touch, but who will build up what you pull down?"[6]

Voltaire, also noted for his rude and unconventional behavior, had evidently been taken more brusquely to task for a similar social outrage, for he wrote caustically to M. le Comte d'Autry (Sept. 6, 1765) that it seemed there was a new kind of *surtout* where you were "forbidden to eat the fruit." He remarked petulantly that he thought it very uncivil for a host to put food before a guest if it was not to be eaten. If one had to "battle over a citron" and make an ignominious and insincere apology *(faire une paix plâtrée)*, it might be worse than open warfare.

Well-bred guests apparently were content to admire the rare fruits and sweetmeats in the *surtout* or the epergne without touching them, awed by the knowledge that these delicacies could only have been procured in small quantities and at great expense. Considering the epergne as a treasury for the choicest morsels, one can begin to see a connection between the *épargne* and the medieval ewer. This association is not because of the ewer's spout but because in the Middle Ages, ewers and other utensils of gold or silver were literally displayed on the buffet as in a treasury, for they represented the wealth and power of their important owner. Money in this form was easy to keep an eye on (banks being non-existent) or to carry away in time of siege. Then too, the valuable objects could be melted down if necessary to provide a daughter with a royal dowry.

Another possible clue to the implications of this term is that in medieval days, according to Victor Gay, the word *épargne* was used by enamelers in the sense of "reserve." The term *taille d'épargne* (which means cut, with something saved or in reserve) was used in regard to champlevé enamel, in which the surface of the metal is cut out in all the places destined to receive the enamel while other areas, such as the lines of the design or larger contrasting areas, are left uncut. In addition to their decorative purpose these uncut areas form a necessary barrier which prevents the various colors of the enamels from running into each other when being fired. This use of the word *épargne* therefore substantiates the idea of something protected and set apart as was the fruit in the epergne.

Whatever the origin of the word, English silversmiths and their elite customers were greatly intrigued with the idea of this grandly pyramidal ornament with its swinging baskets for fruit or flowers. Charming versions appeared in ceramics and glass as well as in silver, and mid-18th-century designs in all materials were awash with rococo curves, shell forms, and sprightly interpretations of chinoiserie (Plate 69). At the end of the century classic taste prevailed and exuberance was sobered, the baskets often taking the serene contours of the Greek *cantharus* (Plate 70). When romanticism became the fashion, mid- and late 19th-century versions were made in naturalistic aspect, with trumpet vases at the top becoming calla lilies or morning-glories and the supporting stand entwined with stems and foliage realistically executed to the last detail (Plate 71).

All this happened in England. One looks in vain for anything resembling the epergne in France until the late 19th century when French variants of the English ones did occasionally appear.

In France the development of table centerpieces followed quite a different pattern. By the time that Louis XIV's edicts had all been repealed in the early 18th century, making silver again available for luxury items like the *surtout-de-table,* the fashionable world could not have cared less. A few silver centerpieces, of course, were made (Plate 72), but the great enthusiasm now was for the exciting new porcelain which so delightfully lent itself to fresh, imaginative conceptions of the *surtout-de-table* (Plate 73). The greatly increased production of mirror glass and its use as a base or plateau for porcelain ornaments was also a factor contributing to the new material's popularity, for the mirror added the brilliant sparkle so much admired. Porcelain figures, classic temples, three-tiered dessert stands, and candelabra beautifully coordinated in design all reflected in the mirror with dazzling charm. The dessert was now "dressed out" in this new manner, with the fruits and sweetmeats adding their quota of form and color, the mirror felicitously making the rare imported fruits look like "more."

The popular three-tiered dessert stand, the French version of the epergne, was taller and more slender than the epergne and was not usually placed in the center of the plateau but displayed in pairs as an integral part of the whole *surtout-de-table*. The latter now fully lived up to its name, being truly "above everything" on the table in beauty, importance, and extent.

The French *surtout,* and those of other European countries which followed the French fashion, naturally changed in style from one period to another as

PLATE 67: "The Burghley Nef." A nautilus shell is mounted in silver and parcel gilt and rests on a silver mermaid's back. It was made by Pierre le Flamand in Paris in 1482–83, and came to England in the 19th century as part of the French inheritance of the then Marchioness of Exeter. (*Victoria & Albert Museum, London, Crown Copyright*)

PLATE 68: Surtout-de-table by Bernhard Heinrich Weye. Though exuberantly rococo in mid-18th-century style, this German surtout is similar in plan to those of the 17th century because of its free-standing casters and condiment dishes, 1757–59 (see detail of this surtout, Plate 139). *(Courtesy, Wadsworth Athenaeum, Hartford)*

PLATE 69: English silver epergne. This chinoiserie epergne was made by Thomas Pitts, 1762–63. *(Courtesy, Colonial Williamsburg, Virginia)*

PLATE 70: Classic Revival silver epergne with baskets in the shape of the Greek cantharus; English silver, 1790. *(Museum of Fine Arts, Boston)*

PLATE 71: A naturalistic glass epergne, late 19th century. This piece was used in a Victorian setting at the London Flower Arrangement Festival in July, 1959. The containers are typical of the period, and the geranium leaves are arranged in flat arabesques reminiscent of John Perkins' 1877 designs. *(Arrangement by Mrs. Rita Maxted)*

PLATE 72: Louis XV dessert stand, mid-18th century. The easy grace and spirited rhythm of the rococo style is perfectly exemplified in this charming dessert stand of silver gilt, probably a corner piece of a large surtout-de-table. The shell forms so much used account for the name rococo, from "rocaille," meaning rock and shell. *(Wellesley College Art Museum; gift of Mrs. Albert M. Steinert in memory of her daughter, Kathryn L. Steinert, class of 1928)*

PLATE 73: Mythological subjects and Greek legends were popular in mid-18th century. This Meissen centerpiece, representing "The Judgment of Paris," is an example of the new way of using porcelain as table decoration. *(Courtesy, Wadsworth Athenaeum, Hartford)*

PLATE 74: Washington's surtout-de-table in the dining room at Mt. Vernon. Seen here are the surviving sections of the original nine "glasses" (the silver-railed mirror plateau) with one of the three classic groups of French biscuit porcelain in the center. *(Courtesy, Mt. Vernon Ladies' Association of the Union, Virginia)*

PLATE 75: Surtout on a Christmas table. For a Christmas party in a Classic Revival mansion on Beacon Hill, Boston, a gay little surtout was constructed in the manner of cartonage, topped by a tiny tree made of eucalyptus "roses" and surrounded by a wreath of gilded holly and mistletoe. Christmas tree ornaments in the shape of tiny fruits were on stands at either end, and a mirror plateau reflected the colorful baubles. *(Arrangement by the author at the Women's City Club, Boston; photograph by Zitso Studio)*

did the English epergne. As porcelain figures were expensive, many ornaments for the plateau were made of sugar, either as the chief figurines or as an architectural or gardenesque background for a few porcelain ones. Rococo arabesques of sugar are illustrated with "Chinese" figures on a plateau in *Le Cannameliste Français* (Plate 84), while during the Classic Revival, Greek temples and mythological figures of sugar are recommended to adorn the plateau.

In these United States between 1789 and 1792 President George Washington carried on an extensive correspondence with various friends likely to be in Paris, asking them to purchase for him a *surtout* complete with "table ornaments" similar to those he had seen on the tables of Robert Morris of Philadelphia and the French and Spanish ambassadors. At last, through the efforts of Gouverneur Morris, he acquired the coveted "images" which were fine classic groups of figures in French biscuit porcelain. But he still lacked a proper set of "glasses" for their display, by which he meant a fashionable mirror and silver plateau made in sections so that the size of the *surtout* could be adjusted to the number of the guests. As Washington wrote to Clement Biddle, he had a Frenchman in his household "who is said to be a compleat confectioner, and professes to understand everything relative to those ornaments, so that the Glasses only are wanting."[7]

Today, on the dining table at Mt. Vernon, we can see the mirror plateau which Mr. Morris purchased for the President (or, at least a few sections of the original nine) with its handsome railing of silver and, in the center, one of the French porcelain groups depicting Aphrodite and two cupids (Plate 74). The pair of side "groups" and the twelve small figures which have also miraculously survived are privately owned. Apparently not surviving are the two vases which Gouverneur Morris describes in his journal, written within a few days of the purchase of these ornaments, with the additional note that "when occasion serves the Tops may be laid aside and the vases filled with natural flowers."

If we would picture this elegant table as set for Washington on a State occasion, we must remember that it was adorned not only with the three biscuit-porcelain groups, the two vases, and the twelve smaller figures on the plateau. Perhaps there also were further ornaments of sugar, exhibiting the skill of his "compleat" French confectioner who may have provided artificial or sugar flowers for the vases when "natural" ones were not available.

In the late 18th century the fashion for a *surtout-de-table* became more and more widespread, and those who could not afford biscuit porcelain and a galleried mirror plateau were able to rent or buy very attractive ones of inexpensive material from the confectioner. (Plate 75 shows *surtout* for contemporary Christmas table; see also Plate 149 for early 19th-century example.) The pyramidal form still prevailed, in the three- or four-tiered fruit stands, and details of crystal prisms, garlands of glass beads, carved figures, and gilded-and-embossed borders made a brave show. The few that have survived are collectors' items today and command a considerable price.

In 1790, however, when purchasing the ornaments for Washington's plateau, Gouverneur Morris was far too astute to buy anything of this sort despite Washington's cautious "Direction as to Oeconomy." When Morris wrote to him from Paris to justify the high price of the classic "images" of biscuit porcelain, he explained, "I could have sent you a Number of pretty Trifles, but . . . your Table would have been in the Style of a *petite Maitresse* of this City, which most assuredly is not the Style you wish . . . I think it of very great Importance to fix the taste of our Country properly, and I think your Example will go very far in that Respect. It is therefore my Wish that every Thing about you should be substantially good and majestically plain; made to endure."[8]

❧ SEVEN

Images & Garden-Parterre Centerpiece

IN THE 18th century it was the height of fashion to make the table look "not like a table at all but like a garden parterre." Whole sets of figures with accompanying artificial trees, fountains, urns, and other garden ornaments (Plates 78 and 79) were sold to be assembled on the mirror plateau, their elegance and extent varying according to the taste and resources of the host or hostess.

Sometimes at a very grand party, the whole *surtout* might be made of porcelain—the plateau itself, the figures, or "images" as they were called, flowers, trees, and all accessories. But the more porcelain, the more prohibitive the price, and for people of average wealth the garden effect, at least, was more often contrived with flowers and little trees of silk or curled paper, or with real flowers dipped in white of egg and sugar to give a surface which sparkled like porcelain.

Architectural features of a fashionable garden including trellis work, Greek temples, and Chinese railings were also added. Toward the end of the century when every fine garden boasted of at least one classic temple, this was the most favored ornament for the table as well. It provided a suitable shelter for a porcelain Pomona, goddess of fruit, an Aphrodite, or a Flora and made an imposing center or "corner piece" in effective contrast to the smaller objects.

Those who could not afford "images" of porcelain (or of silver gilt which was a close second in terms of extravagance and desirability) could buy charming ones of glass, made by enamelers in the technique known as "lamp work," derived from Italy but brought to greatest perfection at Nevers in central France in the 17th and 18th centuries (Plates 80 and 81). Even the whole garden parterre—on its own plateau and complete with little glass trees, fountains, vases of flowers, and urns on pedestals—could be purchased and some of these have even survived to the present day. Delightful Venetian examples are on display at the Murano Museum of Glass, near Venice, and an enchanting one of *verre de Nevers,* with figures as well as a fountain and other garden ornaments, may be seen at the Musée des Arts Décoratifs in Paris.

Separate "images" or groups of men, women, animals, trees, flowers, and other accessories of Nevers glass were sold by the dozen[1] and could be attached to a mirror plateau with "green wax" according to individual fancy. Not as prohibitive in price as porcelain, they were made and imitated in great numbers and would have provided a garden centerpiece of considerable charm.

Still less affluent followers of fashion had to content themselves with "dessert frames" (as they were called in England), furnished by the confectioner. These had wax figures dressed in silk, or sugar figures made to look as much like porcelain as possible. Every skilled confectioner could, of course, furnish even a classic temple of sugar if necessary. Other craftsmen too took up the fad for temples, making delightful ones in all sorts of materials: pottery, glass, marble, ebony, or rosewood. Makers of *cartonage* (architectural constructions in gilded or embossed cardboard) produced inexpensive replicas of them and these were sold or rented by confectioners (Fig. 7 and Plate 82). Savary des Bruslons, in his *Dictionaire . . . de Commerce* (1759), says that Seguin, the French maker of artificial flowers, catered to this trade and not only made flowers and little trees for table parterres but also *cartonage* trellises with artificial vines. One may assume that he made *cartonage* temples as well.

In order to maintain any status whatsoever, it is obvious that some sort of a miniature garden for the center of the table had to be achieved. Even in America the fashion was known, if not widely prevalent, for an advertisement in the *Boston Gazette* as early as 1757 offered "a complete Set of Dessert Frames, with Arbours, Alcoves, Hedging, China Flower Pots etc. with spare Grass and Gravel for ditto."[2]

The reason for this fashion is not hard to find. Enthusiasm for gardens and gardening was then an obsession. Gentlemen enjoyed "projecting" designs for their own gardens, and Wedgwood referred to this fashion as "a universal madness." In the light of this *furor hortensis,* nothing could be more logical than to provide a garden setting for the new "images" so much admired. The vogue

FIGURE 7: Confectioner's trade card advertising a cartonage temple and images, 18th century. *(From Les Accessoires du Costume et du Mobilier by H. d'Allemagne, 1928)*

for the garden-parterre centerpiece conformed, of course, to whatever happened to be the latest fashion in garden design. The Renaissance garden was severely symmetrical; 17th-century France enlivened symmetrical compartments with designs like embroidery patterns, worked, not with flowers, but with colored earths or sand (Plate 83). In mid-century, "embroidered parterres" became asymmetrical, employing rococo arabesques (Plate 84), while under the Classic Revival, there was a return to strict symmetry only to be followed by naturalistic, romantic patterns. All these forms were reflected in turn on the table parterre, even to the point of making miniature embroidered parterres with colored sugar, known to confectioners as "sand." Sometimes the designs were made with tiny candies called *nonpareilles* or with powdered marble dust tinted to procure "les nuances." White of egg kept the designs from blowing away.[3]

In the late 18th and early 19th centuries, although there was much controversy over the merits of the formal classic parterre versus the asymmetrical "English" or naturalistic garden, both were fashionable. Often in real gardens the two styles were combined in an amusing and rather incongruous way, and this was equally true of the garden-like centerpiece. Kew Gardens, predominantly Romantic, had several classic temples but otherwise went all out for the naturalistic style with its clumps of shrubbery, serpentine paths, and Chinese pagoda, as did many another garden of the 18th and early 19th century not only in England but also on the Continent. Similarly, no one remarked any inconsistency in a silver fountain at the head of the Prince Regent's table at an evening party at Carleton Palace in 1811, although the rest of the garden centerpiece was completely rustic. "A purling stream of pure water down the center of the supper table" emerged from this rather formal fountain and "fell in a cascade at the outlet. The mimic banks were adorned with moss and flowers and small gold and silver fish were seen glistering here and there in the stream, which was crossed at intervals with little fantastic bridges."[4]

Whether formal or informal, rococo, romantic, or classic, or a little of each, these fluctuations in style never for a moment dimmed the popularity of the parterre centerpiece from the beginning of the 18th well into the 19th century. But the idea did not spring fully formed, like Athena from the head of Zeus, in the 18th century, although to be sure it was then that it reached its extravagant zenith. It took a long time developing and defining itself from its archtype, the gardenesque "entremet" or conversation piece, which had appeared as early as the 15th century.

There was that flowery pleasance on the table of the Comte du Maine in 1455, when "the center of the table was like a green meadow surrounded with flowering branches to which violets and other sweet smelling flowers had been attached." Another medieval description tells of a table that was "decorated with the Vine, so that the guests could see the very grapes while they were drinking the wine." This table, according to Le Grand d'Aussy, is mentioned in the poetry of Fortunatus (6th century) and was of "very artistic workmanship" which indicates that the design was either painted on the surface or worked in metal. The historian comments that Charlemagne had three similar tables made of massy silver "even more remarkable for their workmanship than for their material." The grapevine theme seems to have been a popular one for some time, as a very beautiful tabletop, painted in Germany in the 16th century, is now in the National Museum at Munich. The design consists of verdure and animals very freely and casually painted with huge bunches of grapes in the center, much larger than the deer, swans, birds, monkeys, and other creatures entwined in the foliage.

Similar flights of fancy with a garden theme may have appeared on other important early tables, and their playful spirit can well inspire us with ideas for conversation pieces on informal tables today. A centerpiece suggested by the 15th-century "green meadow" was made for Margaret Fairbanks Marcus's book, *Period Flower Arrangement* using a frolicsome pottery stag in a setting of flowering mosses, rocks, and "trees" enclosed by a wattle fence of lilac whips, on an oval pewter platter. This centerpiece did not attempt to be authentically medieval but used the description of the Comte du Maine's table to spark a contemporary interpretation, resulting in a gay and sprightly decoration for an informal luncheon in early spring (Plate 85). Another centerpiece, this time mindful of that table "decorated with the Vine," was made recently for a Harvest Supper. Branches of an old gnarled grapevine, laid on the table, encircled the centerpiece, and where they arched high enough above the surface of the table, great bunches of black Hamburg grapes were hung with dramatic effect as they came close to the saffron-colored burlap which simulated a homespun cloth. Simple earthenware and thick, out-sized goblets used as hurricane shields for candles suggested medieval textures and contours, and low wicker baskets of fruit and flowers followed Roman and medieval counterparts (Plate 76).

Still another table comes to mind which, though not inspired by a medieval description, was nevertheless medieval in spirit. It was made some years ago for an important State Garden Federation luncheon in Columbus, Georgia and had the charm of a spring woodland scene. Large groups of King Alfred daffodils were arranged as if growing amid rocks and mossy logs, with naturalistic pools of water being cleverly contrived at intervals all down the center of the head table. To heighten this mood of spring enchantment, a pair of delightful "life-sized" elves, made of papier-mâché and borrowed from the display department of a local shop, perched cross legged on huge "mushrooms" at either end. Every last detail contributed to the effectiveness of this spring fantasy. The tablecloths were of moss green burlap, the napkins of wood brown linen and, with groups of the same daffodils arranged naturalistically on all the smaller tables, the whole room (in reality a rather bare and barnlike "hall") created the impression of a garden in the woods. It was unforgettable.

Descriptions of garden centerpieces during the Renaissance indicate that they were still admired as an innovation but had abandoned the naïve medieval use of "whatever Nature offered to the eye" and depended more upon "the inventions of art" to induce comment. At the banquet concluding the week of festivities celebrating the wedding of Charles the Bold, Duke of Burgundy, in 1468, when the influence of the Italian Renaissance was just beginning to reach northern Europe, the banquet table described by Olivier de La Marche had "thirty plateaux in the manner of gardens" in which no real fruit or flowers appeared. Instead they seem to have been little masterpieces of the goldsmith's art. The bases of the plateaux of brazilwood (a bright red wood from an Asiatic tree from which, it is reported, Brazil was named) were bordered with "hedges" of silver, the principal one, presumably larger and in the center, being "hedged with gold." In the midst of the plateau was a large golden tree, and "against this tree was the Meat."

According to the chronicler, every plateau had its tree, "of all other sorts of which the fruits and flowers are so cleverly made that they seem to be real trees and real fruits and are very beautiful to see." Figures were set about these trees, "men, as well as women, all decorated with gold, silver, and silk. They have divers activities; some appear to be throwing sticks to knock down the fruit, and others have long staves for the same purpose. Some women hold out their hats to receive the fruits and others stretch out their hands with a pleased expression."[5] The same idea is present in 18th-century versions (Plate 80).

Baron van der Elst, in *The Last Flowering of the Middle Ages,* says that several famed artists were summoned to Bruges to design the decorations for the duke's wedding, including Jacques Daret and Hugo van der Goes, and that the latter is known to have worked ten and a half days on the decorations for the wedding. Possibly even the great Memling himself, who lived in Bruges was also employed on the project, and the designs may have been carried out by one of the many skilled Flemish goldsmiths of the 15th century. One may well imagine that these thirty plateaux "in the manner of gardens" were truly "beautiful to see."

Olivier de La Marche also describes another banquet decoration (at the Chateau de Lille in 1454), which was quoted recently in *Antiques* magazine by Paul Perrot, Director of the Corning Museum of Glass. On the table as a conversation piece there was "a very beautiful fountain, partly in glass and partly in lead of a very new aspect, for there were small trees made of glass with marvelous leaves and flowers; and in an empty space, as in a clearing, surrounded by rocks, there was a small St. Andrew standing erect with his cross in front of him."[6] This, Mr. Perrot says, must have been "one of the earliest descriptions of what may be called a typical verre de Nevers tableau," though made long before Nevers was to owe its renown to the little glass figurines. That there was a glassmaker in Lille sufficiently skilled in this technique to provide this little fountain was most unusual at this date.

One wonders if it could have been due to the brisk trade which flourished between Italy and Burgundy in the 15th century. Perhaps a defecting Venetian glassworker, or, more likely, one from the less strict Altare factory joined the train of Arnolfini or of some other dealer carrying Italian luxuries to the north and thus brought this distinctive new technique to Lille.

If the Italians brought ideas as well as goods and services to Burgundy, they may also have taken note of a few Burgundian innovations. Portinari, the wealthy Florentine banker, led the procession of Florentine guests at the wedding of Charles the Bold. He and his fellow citizens among those present must have seen the "plateaux in the manner of gardens" at the wedding banquet and could have introduced this new and captivating fashion at home.

At any rate, by the end of the 16th century the idea seems to be sufficiently established in Italy to appear in a rather routine book on a minor branch of household management. *Il Trinciante* (He Who Carves Meat for the Table) was published in Rome in 1593, and one of its illustrations, which seems to have nothing to do with carving, shows a fantastic centerpiece (Plate 86). It is surrounded by a "hedge" of closely bound foliage, fruit, and flowers and has two men fishing in a similarly bordered pool and assorted animals tethered securely to the trunks of eight stiff little trees. Whether these figures, not to mention the trees, the tufts of flowers between, and the animals—four dogs, a rabbit, a deer, a sheep, and a hedgehog—were made of glass, pottery, or sugar is not divulged, but the illustrations in a book of this kind probably represented a more or less familiar form of decoration to be carried out in whatever material was available.

According to Mme. d'Aulnoy, a French writer of fairy tales who also wrote books on travel, the fashion for sugared ornaments in the manner of gardens came from Italy. She describes a party at the archbishop's palace in Toledo: "As for the dessert it was the best and even the most diverting thing that one could see, for they had glacéed in sugar whole little trees, in the fashion of Italy; you may well imagine that the trees were very small. There were orange trees candied in this manner, with some little birds made and attached on top. Cherry trees, strawberry plants, currants and still others each in a little silver pot."[7]

Thus the garden centerpiece idea traveled from one country to another, gradually gaining in favor throughout Europe as time went on. Every century from its introduction in the late Middle Ages on seems to have played with the conceit, adapting it to existing materials and relating it to prevailing fashions in garden design. But the real impetus which transformed it into a veritable furor probably came out of Meissen in Germany where the secret of making true porcelain was discovered at the beginning of the 18th century.

At first the Meissen factory made porcelain in styles suggested by Chinese wares and silversmiths' work, but designers were soon captivated by the possibilities of the exciting new material for fresh artistic expressions. While it was necessary to satisfy the demands of Augustus the Strong (Elector of Saxony, and King of Poland, who sponsored the Meissen factory), for huge vases and colossal porcelain figures which he had a passion for using like sculpture in his Dresden palace, it was also imperative to make some smaller, income-producing ornaments as well, and delightfully painted tablewares soon found a ready market at luxury-loving European courts. Charming little figures were made to take the place of those of wax or sugar which had long been fashionable as ornaments for the dessert. When Herold, a gifted artist and skilled technician, came to the factory in 1720, he soon capitalized upon the prevailing vogue for chinoiserie and became famous for his Chinese figures and "Indian flowers" taken from designs on Oriental porcelains.

The fashion for using these figures on the table parterre was further exploited by a curious circumstance. It so happened that the Count de Brühl, who became director of the Meissen (Dresden) porcelain factory in 1723 after the death of Augustus the Strong, had a special predilection for huge and fantastic dessert services. *Surtouts-de-table* of vast proportions and extraordinary originality were designed for the count by Kaëndler, another master modeler at Meissen who had been trained as a sculptor and had also a gift for architectural invention, making him well equipped to deal with the new porcelain on a large scale.

In the lordly fashion of the day, the Count de Brühl made a convenient arrangement with the factory whereby a large percentage of its production was made according to his specifications and for his own use. Though a costly plan from the factory's point of view, this proved in the end to be a successful form of publicity. Many a European visitor of wealth and importance admired and remarked upon these extraordinary centerpieces when entertained at the count's table, and the fashion for similar extravaganzas in the new Saxon china became the rage. In 1748 Sir Charles Hanbury Williams, the English Ambassador at the court of Augustus III, describes a party given by the count "where we sat down at one table two hundred and six people. When the dessert was set on, I thought it was the most wonderful thing I ever beheld. I fancied myself either in a garden or at the Opera. But I could not imagine that I was at dinner. In the middle of the table was the fountain of the Piazza Navona at Rome, at least eight feet high, which ran all the while with rose water, and tis said that piece alone cost six thousand dollars."[8]

The ambassador was more enthusiastic than accurate, for this table fountain has since been identified as a replica not of the Roman fountain but of one in the count's own garden in Dresden, designed by the Italian, Mattielli. We do not know the actual size of the central group of this splendid dessert service, but parts of it are now in the Victoria and Albert Museum in London, including one gleaming white porcelain table fountain about two and a half feet high accompanied by a pair of magnificently winged horses and two enormous white covered urns. This group may have constituted a mere "corner piece" to the great central one admired by the ambassador, or in his amazement he may have slightly exaggerated the measurements. Of course he could have reckoned from the floor up! At any rate, one can easily picture the astonishment of the guests at this dramatic use of the sparkling new material (Plate 87).

Many attractive if less spectacular figures and gardenesque ornaments were made not only at Meissen but also in other European factories where the secret formula for porcelain had been discovered via workmen defecting from the Meissen factory. European factories still not possessed of the secret of true porcelain made similar ornaments of soft paste porcelain, then considered inferior but today held in highest esteem. All were in demand for table "gardens," and even dishes not on the plateau were often in naturalistic forms of leaves, flowers, fruits, and vegetables (Plate 121). The Chelsea factory in England advertised "cupids for the Desart," and the Vincennes factory sponsored by Mme. de Pompadour excelled in vases of porcelain flowers. The Vincennes flowers, though of soft paste porcelain, were even in their own day acknowledged to be superior and were often used to embellish Meissen vases and candelabra. "Images" of course were the greatest rage and were made everywhere in both types of porcelain.

But by the end of the 18th century the magic of porcelain had worn off. Still expensive but without that early quality of "newness," rarity, and wonder, it had lost much of its initial appeal. Then too, the abrupt change in fashion from the exuberant rococo to the severe classic style called for less fluid shapes and more sober textures. Honey says that Wedgwood, who had made delightful rococo table ornaments in his famous creamware, became a devoted classicist and now "turned from porcelain as from something evil, tainted with Orientalism and frivolity." He made centerpieces in the garden-parterre manner but used his newly invented jasper ware with a matte finish, embellished with classic detail (Plate 88). His black *basaltes* ware was also dull in finish, while some of his earthenware simulated granite or marble. All of these new textures were deemed more suited to the dignified sobriety of classic taste prevailing.

Throughout all its vicissitudes, however, the parterre centerpiece survived. It is still vital and alluring, for at lavish debutante dinners and other festive and extravagant parties we often see contemporary versions of the idea. When a dinner table "in the 18th-century manner" is called for, as often happens in our flower shows, what an agreeable surprise it would be if an exhibitor were to execute a garden parterre with delicacy and charm (Plate 77). It would be far more authoritative as a centerpiece than the usual "Georgian" or "French 18th-century" bouquet derived from flower paintings or prints of the period which, however beautiful, show a type of arrangement which probably never appeared on an 18th-century table.

PLATE 76: Table "decorated with the Vine," suggested by a medieval description. Fruit is arranged in pyramids on basket lids, as in Plate 57. (*Arrangement by the author; photograph by Zitso Studio*)

PLATE 77: Cartonage temple and garden parterre at a Garden Club of America dinner in 1961. The temple, cache-pots, and candy dishes—all of cartonage—were made by Mrs. Albert C. Burrage, Jr. The carnation "trees" and hedge in French glass rivieres were arranged by the author. *(Photograph by Francis Lambert)*

PLATE 78: Temples and garden hedges with images on a Dutch table in 1768. *(From a fete book by Jan Wagenaar, 1709–73, with engravings by Simon Fokke; courtesy, Prints Division, New York Public Library)*

PLATE 79: A magnificent dessert. Temples, pyramids of fruit, and sugar ornaments are seen on a 1717 German table. Note the high-backed chairs and the general atmosphere of informality at the end of a party. *(Engraving from* Deutsches Leben der Vergangenheit in Bildern *by E. Diederichs, Jena, 1908)*

PLATE 80: The Cherry Pickers, in 18th-century glass. This French piece, possibly from Nevers, may have been part of a set of similar groups made for the mirror plateau. The subject harks back to the 15th century when "thirty plateaux in the manner of gardens" with groups of figures picking fruit ornamented the Duke of Burgundy's table. (*Art Institute of Chicago; gift of Mrs. Potter Palmer*)

PLATE 81: "Winter," an 18th-century figure of Nevers glass. Although only seven inches tall, the figure is endowed with astonishing personality and glacial mien. Originally, no doubt, he was accompanied by the more appealing but equally expressive figures of spring, summer, and autumn. "The Seasons" ornamented the dessert plateau, just as such figures of stone or marble ornamented a real garden. (*Victoria & Albert Museum, London, Crown Copyright*)

PLATE 82: Temple for the center of the table. This is a temple of gilded and embossed cardboard, ornamented with garlands and artificial flowers. *(An 18th-century trade card, from* Les Accessoires du Costume et du Mobilier *by d'Allemagne)*

PLATE 83. A typical "embroidered parterre" in a 17th-century garden. *(Engraving by Perelle; Print Department, Metropolitan Museum of Art; Rogers Fund, 1920)*

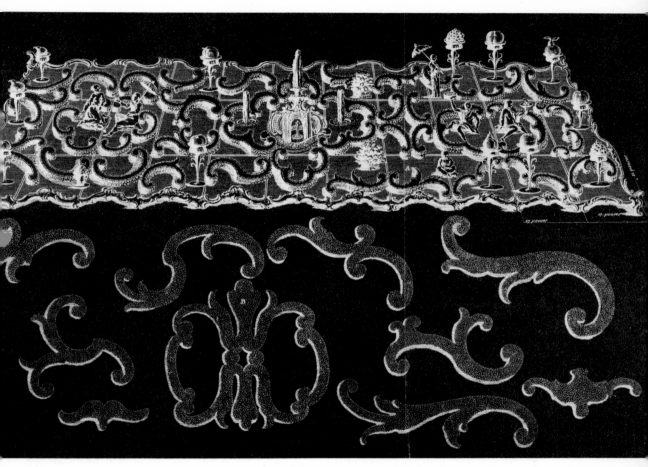

PLATE 84. Rococo table parterre with figures and arabesques of
sugar. Note the single specimens of fruit in tall goblets and the
patterns for sugar hedges in foreground. *(From* Le Cannameliste
Français *by Gilliers, Chef d'Office to the King of Poland, 1751; courtesy,
Harvard College Library)*

PLATE 85: Green Meadow centerpiece. Sprigs of sumac, blueberry and sweet fern, with rocks, flowering mosses, and early wild flowers made a centerpiece suggested by a 15th-century description. (From Period Flower Arrangement by Margaret Fairbanks Marcus; arrangement by the author; photograph by Zitso Studio; courtesy of M. Barrows & Co.)

PLATE 86: Fish pond centerpiece from an Italian treatise on carving; Rome, 1593. (Print Department, Metropolitan Museum of Art, New York; Dick Fund)

PLATE 87: Meissen table fountain by Kaëndler of winged horses and urns. This is part of the extraordinary dessert service which Sir Charles Hanbury Williams saw on the table of the Count de Brühl in Dresden in the 18th century. *(Victoria & Albert Museum, London, Crown Copyright)*

PLATE 88: Blue-and-white Wedgwood parterre centerpiece, 1851.
Note the candelabra, compotes, and small tazze on plinths. The
bases of the candelabra have metal liners for flowers, and flowers
may also have been used in the small urns which ornament the
balustrade of the mirror plateau. The length is 7 feet, 7 inches.
(Courtesy, Jean Gorely, secretary of the Wedgwood Club, Boston)

PLATE 89: Fruit on black plates. Fruit is served at a casual luncheon for two in an artist's living room. This time an antique Chinese pottery cat, decked with a spray of fresh stephanotis is used as centerpiece. *(Courtesy of Mrs. Edward F. Bowman; photograph by Francis Lambert)*

PLATE 90: A stylish and effortless arrangement. Large black Hamburg grapes are still rare things today and worthy of being displayed on a Canton compote. Handsome autumn leaves (these of the buttonwood tree, Platanus occidentalis) may be waxed and pressed to be used in winter to set off any fine fruit. *(Arrangement by the author; photograph by Zitso Studio)*

EIGHT

Fruits for the Dessert

A GROUP OF triumphant French skin divers and archaeologists were having a unique banquet on the deck of the research ship "Calypso" in the Mediterranean in May of 1953. Divers, scientists, and crew were in Greek costume, and the table was set with ancient black Campanian pottery dishes which they had just finished salvaging from the hold of a ship that had foundered some two thousand years before off its intended port near Marseilles. The Greek ship's cargo of dishes had been made by Greek potters living in the region of Campania in southern Italy around 230 B.C.

Television cameras were at the ready, for the banquet had been planned as a publicity stunt to create interest and raise additional funds for the project, and the men, quite willing to celebrate after a winter of exhausting and dangerous work, were gay and exuberant over their Greek banquet. But as the meal progressed, it had for them a far deeper meaning than a celebration of the return of spring and of a difficult task accomplished.

As the leader of the salvaging operation, Jacques-Yves Cousteau (French naval officer and co-inventor of the Cousteau-Gagnon aqualung) wrote, "The Greek banquet in the open air became a communion with the past, hilarious with wine and high feelings but with a meaning that none could escape. The Campanian dishes had arrived at the customer's table." There was a sudden appreciation, too, among the celebrants, of the refinement of Greek taste as they noticed that the black plates brought out the beauty of fruit and other foods and "mustard spread in a small dish became nectar." One little bowl, whose use could not at first be determined, they filled with olives. It was "the perfect olive dish," and the divers believed it must have been so employed by the Greeks themselves.[1]

Through the centuries craftsmen other than Greeks have discovered that food set forth in handsome bowls and dishes adds much to the enjoyment of a fine meal and so have devoted their talents to designing for this lucrative market. Particularly is this true of dishes designed for fruit, the customary dessert for centuries. Some of the most beautiful appointments in the history of table decoration have been made for the service of the dessert, and since fruit was available in most countries in considerable variety, it was the logical thing to serve at the end of a hearty meal due to its welcome lightness and astringent freshness.

In Egypt and in the East many exotic fruits abounded. Thomas Coryate, an indefatigable English traveler in the early 17th century, visited India where he stayed many months with the British Ambassador and was an intimate friend of the ambassador's chaplain, the Rev. Edward Terry. Michael Strachan, in *The Life and Adventures of Thomas Coryate,* draws upon Terry's memoirs for additional details of life in India at that time and tells us that "the Ambassador's household reveled in melons, pomegranates, lemons, oranges, dates, figs, grapes, bananas, mangoes and even pineapples introduced into India from America by the Portuguese and tasting, as Terry puts it, 'like strawberries, claret wine, rose water and sugar well tempered together.'"

In Italy, southern France, and Spain many of these same fruits were grown, and in northern Europe fruits suited to cooler climates were cultivated from the time of Charlemagne. In the Middle Ages dried fruits were imported into Europe from the Orient, while fruits locally available were preserved in brandy or sugar so that the dessert at all seasons, even in the north, presented a colorful display and could be served with imagination and distinction on the "grand table."

The idea of black dishes as a stunning foil for fruit had been appreciated by more than one craftsman even before the days of the Campanian potters. Black wares were made in ancient times in Egypt; in Iran and later in the Sung dynasty of China (960–1279). Mexico, among other countries, excels in the production of black pottery. In England, Wedgwood in the 18th century was inspired by Greek and Etruscan examples when he invented his famous black *basaltes,* as he called his fine, hard-finished black ware because of its resemblance to the natural stone of that name. (True to the classicism of his day he used the Latin form of the English word, basalt.) Some of the best modern potters and craftsmen in glass and enameled copper often make black or nearly black bowls and plates in subtle shapes not unlike those seen in ancient pottery. Clever shopkeepers sometimes put a few oranges or persimmons in one of those on display to call attention to their decorative possibilities.

There have been many other ways of enhancing the beauty of fruit. In a fresco of the 1st century from the Roman Villa Boscoreale is a lovely glass bowl filled with fruit (Plate 92). Both bowl and fruits have similar plump, rounded contours, and the fruit is further set off by clusters of its own foliage. From early Roman days also comes the familiar shell form so popular through succeeding centuries for the display of fruit, whether in glass, silver, or porcelain. During the Renaissance that great lover of factual detail, Ghirlandaio, presents us with a superb charger of fruit garnished with flowers, as does Titian in the portrait said to be of his daughter, Lavinia. Dutch and Flemish still-life painters of the 17th century loved to show fruit in handsome delft earthenware made to look as much as possible like the Chinese porcelains which, though fabulously expensive, were used for high pyramids of fruit at the extravagant entertainments of kings and princes.

In the 17th century the word "fruit" was often used broadly to include jellies, "sweetmeats," syllabubs, cheese, nuts, ices, and *dragées,* as well as actual fruit. *Dragées* were tiny candies made in pretty, fanciful shapes filled with nuts or liqueurs. Even in the Middle Ages *dragées* had been an admired feature of the dessert. Sweetmeats were tarts, candied fruits, or sweet biscuits also formed in an imaginative way, adding to the decorative display. Syllabubs were concoctions of cream and wine. Ices, introduced in the 16th century, were an exciting novelty when they first appeared. Mrs. Beeton, in the 1868 edition of her book of household management, claims that it was Catherine de' Medici who introduced ices. "Will not this fact," says Mrs. Beeton, "cover a multitude of Sins committed by the instigator of St. Bartholomew?"

A list of fruits served at a great feast following the ceremonies of Investiture into the Order of the Garter held in St. George's Hall in 1671 gives an idea of the variety and extent of a typical 17th-century dessert at a grand table:

One Charger of *China Oranges* containing 50
Seven Chargers of *Confections,* in each Charger 20 Boxes; in each Box one pound of dried Confections.

Two Plates of *Duke Cherries,* 4 pounds in each Plate.
One Plate of *Red Strawberries* containing one Gallon,
One Plate of *White Strawberries* containing two Gallons.
One Plate of *Ice Cream*
Three Plates of *Liquid Sweetmeats,* in each Plate 3 pounds.[2]

(Liquid sweetmeats, according to a recipe for "Liquid Apricock Sweetmeats" in *The Professed Cook* by B. Clermont, 1776, were merely stewed fruits and were presumably the same in the 17th century.)

This all-inclusive use of the word "fruit" continued into the 18th and 19th centuries. *Le Cannameliste Français* (1751) defines "fruit" as "that which comprises all the service for the dessert," and in England even today the words "fruit" and "dessert" are still used synonymously.

In the 18th century wealthy noblemen were personally interested in the fine fruits produced by their gardeners, and the "universal madness" over horticulture contributed much to the enthusiasm for new and beautiful varieties. Most frequently mentioned were peaches, pears, strawberries, cherries, and greengage plums. In the 17th century, according to Samuel Pepys, hothouse grapes were "rare things," and in the 18th century, though a little more plentiful, they were still unusual enough in northern countries to warrant special display. But in that age of artificiality, mere rarity was not enough. One must somehow manage to dramatize the presentation, so grapes were often dipped in white of egg and then in powdered sugar to achieve the fashionable *givrage,* or frosty sparkle (Plate 94), or were hung from the ceiling above the table to emphasize their long pendant clusters and call attention to their rarity.

Among exotic fruits raised in 18th-century greenhouses, citrons, bigarades (a bitter orange used for curaçao), and *chinoises* (small oranges which grow abundantly in China), are often mentioned. Small orange trees in porcelain or silver pots, raised in the fashionable orangeries of the late 17th and 18th centuries, were frequently used on the table. With the accession of the Prince of Orange as King William III in 1689, no English courtier's garden could be without orange trees for the terrace or garden parterre (protected during the winter months in nurseries if there was no orangerie), and smaller plants were brought indoors and appropriated for the table "parterre."

With this abundance of the fruits for the dessert, the ways of presenting them were equally various. All three forms of fruit—dried, fresh, and preserved—were offered at one time on a well-supplied table. Much thought was given not only to the effect of the ensemble but also to the disposition of individual specimens, and careful directions were included in 18th-century cookbooks for their correct display. A fresh pear, for example, must always rest on its base with the stem uppermost, whereas apples or oranges could be used either way up. Single, particularly handsome or exotic specimens were sometimes set in tall goblets or champagne glasses and placed as accents (Plate 84) on the mirror plateau. Plums, cherries, strawberries, and other small fruits were either in "moss baskets" or else arranged in pyramidal form on flat compotes, one type of fruit to a container. Candied fruits, however, were not served in pyramids but were carefully arranged in compartmented boxes fitted into huge, round, shallow chargers (Plate 93).

Among these techniques and ingenious containers the importance of the garden-parterre centerpiece as a setting for the dessert must not be forgotten. Not only real fruits meant to be eaten but also artificial fruits were incorporated into its design, and the game of "true or false" provided conversation and amusement. William Coxe, an English tutor on tour in Russia in 1779, describes "china vases at the upper and lower end of the table containing cherry trees in full leaf with fruit hanging on the boughs which was gathered by the company." Although dwarf fruit trees do bear edible fruit, it is hard to believe that even a dwarf cherry tree could be small enough for a table parterre. Probably these trees were artificial and the fruit real.

Baskets, which had been used for centuries for fruit and sweetmeats, were still popular, their shape usually low, oval, and little changed from those of Roman times. They are rather looked down upon, however, by *The Court and Country Cook,* a 1702 version of a French cookbook. Here the author states that they are only used "in preparing Entertainments for certain Fraternities or particular Societies; where as many little baskets are served up to table as there are Guests . . . adorned with small Ribbands and Taffety-covers according to the allotted Expense, and filled up with all sorts of Sweet-meats, Biskits, Marchpanes, Orange and Lemon faggots, dried Fruits etc. so as the most delicious comfits may lye at the top; at last, after all have been set in good Order and contributed much to the Decoration of the Several Courses, every individual Person shuts up and takes away his Basket to treat his Family and Friends at Home."

In the 18th century, in spite of Walpole's assertion that sugar ornaments had been entirely supplanted by Saxon china, they were still included among "the fruits"; however they were quite transformed from the grand and monumental *trionfi* of the 17th century. Those of the now prevailing rococo style were lighthearted and fancifully concocted, following the mode of mid-18th-century porcelain figures and ornaments. Sometimes delicate sugar pyramids composed of openwork arabesques were surmounted by tiny vases of sugar flowers (Plate 62). In the Classic Revival style, at the end of the 18th century, while sugar ornaments preserved an equal delicacy, the wayward curve gave way to classic architectural forms. Parterre beds were rectangular or oval and there were other features of a formal garden—fountains or figures of sylvan nymphs, or "The Seasons," the latter a favorite subject for both garden and table because of Thompson's famous poem of that name (Plate 81). Other popular "images" for the parterre were "The Elements," and "The Continents," whether in sugar, porcelain, or glass.

As for fruits, the great horticultural triumph of the 18th century was the successful cultivation of the pineapple, and its rise to high favor as an ornament for the dessert was phenomenal. This truly exotic fruit came to England and to the Continent by way of the West Indies in the 17th century. After many unsuccessful attempts to bring it to fruition in England's climate, the method of growing it in glass-roofed pits used in Holland was adopted with favorable results. One painting by Hendrick Danckerts (1615–78) shows Rose, the king's gardener, on bended knee presenting the first pineapple grown in England to His Majesty King Charles II. Thenceforth pineapples were raised by those wealthy enough to provide the necessary care and conditions, and a hostess who was fortunate enough to secure one for her dessert was rare indeed.

Anyone possessing such a treasure made sure it would not be overlooked. It might have the place of honor at the top of the epergne or in a pyramid of fruit (Plates 95 and 96), or it might be displayed alone in its glory, standing upright on a tall compote with its green crown aloft (Plate 97). The same pineapple was sometimes observed to be featured at one party after another, and it had to go back to its owner or to the confectioner next day! Horace Walpole, in a letter to Sir Horace Mann on Nov. 12, 1746, described how he once entertained a couple of Italian dignitaries at dinner forgetting that they could not eat meat on a Friday. They took their revenge by consuming the two handsome pineapples which cost a guinea and were intended solely as decoration.

This most admired of all fruits became, for some reason, a symbol of hospitality. Perhaps the fantastic flourish of green leaves sprouting from the top of its intricately patterned golden base suggested the green shoots of friendship. At any rate this association is an old one, as it is said that the Spanish conquerors of South America noted that Peruvian houses on whose gates were carved or wrought pineapples were sure to offer warm hospitality.

The pineapple form invaded many arts. Not only was it used on gate posts and over doorways but, carved in wood, it appeared on bed posts and other furniture. Wedgwood made an epergne with a pineapple at the top in his celebrated creamware, and silversmiths and porcelain makers frequently used its form for finials on the covers of tea pots and sugar bowls. Followers of fashion who could not afford these luxuries had their puddings made in pineapple molds or constructed "pineapples" of daffodils, one of the most ingenious and spectacular methods of arranging daffodils ever devised (Frontispiece). Mme. Calderon de la Barca, the English wife of the Spanish Ambassador to Mexico in the 1830's, describes bouquets made by the Indians "in pineapple or pyramidal form."[3] The "King of Fruits" was having its day indeed.

Nineteenth-century cookbooks, still often referring to the dessert as "the fruit," give explicit directions for the arrangement of the dessert plateau. Hannah Glasse says in 1805 that "every young lady ought to know both how to make all kinds of confectionery and dress out a dessert . . . as it depends wholly on fancy and [demands] but little expence." Carême, famous French confectioner who had served Talleyrand and became *chef de cuisine* to the Prince Regent in England (later King George IV), also maintains that "the dessert ought to be the special labor of the lady of the house." This was not only an admission that not every household had an unlimited staff of servants but also a realization that a light feminine touch and innate taste were needed to give charm and order to what might easily be a meaningless clutter of "little knicknacks" on the table plateau.

It was evident that there was much competition in the matter of presenting an elegant dessert. It seemed to be the ultimate status symbol and early 19th-century cookbooks are full of ideas for the ambitious hostess on how to make her "fruits" the envy of all rivals in the field. Mrs. Beeton, in an 1868 edition of her indispensable book of household management, tells how to construct a dish of mixed fruit (Plate 98). She may have gleaned this idea from the letters of Mrs. Basil Hall who had traveled to America in 1827. Mrs. Hall was not impressed by much, but did condescend to write that the American custom of having various kinds of fruit together in one dish "not only has a prettier effect but prevents the necessity of pulling about the dishes over the table."

Evidently Mrs. Beeton considers this a new idea, even in 1868. She recommends making a dish of mixed fruit by placing a tumbler in the center of the dish, "and in this tumbler, the pine, crown uppermost; round the tumbler put a thick layer of moss and over this apples, pears, plums, peaches and such fruit as is similarly in season." The garnishing needs special attention, she says, "as the contrast of the brilliant-coloured fruits with nicely arranged foliage is very charming." She advises using the double-edged mallow, strawberry, and vine leaves, and for winter desserts "the bay, cuba and laurel are sometimes used." But "the garnish *par excellence* for the dessert is the ice plant [*Mesembryanthemum crystallinum,* called also sea fig and sea marigold] its crystalized dew-drops producing a marvelous effect in the height of summer, giving a most inviting sense of coolness to the fruit it encircles."

In all periods no small contribution to the brilliant "dressing out" of a dessert was made by beautiful table appointments. Dessert services were an important part of household equipment to which in the 18th century the new Saxon china, and the exquisite porcelain soon made elsewhere on the Continent and in England, added a note of luxury and excitement. Mirror plateaux, framed with porcelain, silver, or silver gilt, reflected the lovely forms and colors of the fruit, the sparkle of glass and china, and the dancing flames of wax candles in porcelain, crystal, or silver candelabra. The *givrage* of frosted sugar ornaments, candied grapes or flowers, and tablecloths which might be of silk or silver tissue sprinkled with barley sugar added to the scintillating effect.

Today, fruit, though not inevitably the dessert, is still highly valued for its refreshing qualities and its decorative possibilities, and the hostess continues to search for the perfect dish to enhance its beauty. She may well glean, from earlier methods of display and from the wide range of foliage used as foils, "new" ideas for her own table (Plates 90 and 99).

Only the other day at a reunion of friends who had judged and exhibited at many a flower show together, fruit was presented for dessert in a way that not only satisfied the eye and the palate but also appealed to the diet-conscious as well. Fresh strawberries and long narrow strips of pineapple on modern black lacquer plates from Japan proved Captain Cousteau's assertion that black plates really bring out the beauty of fruit. (Plate 89) The hostess was clever, too, in dodging the flower arrangement issue though she was, herself, many times a blue ribbon winner. The centerpiece on the large round table on this occasion was a magnificent Chinese Export porcelain punch bowl filled with red apples, a casual but effectively inviting conversation piece. Here again, the beauty of the fruit and "the perfect dish" were enough to elicit even from this talented group of guests spontaneous exclamations of delight

PLATE 91: "Still Life," by Francisco de Zurbarán, 1598–1661. Oranges in a basket are crowned with orange blossoms; there are citrons on a silver or pewter plate, and other delightful accessories. *(City Art Museum of St. Louis)*

PLATE 92: Glass bowl of fruit; Roman, 1st century B.C. *(Detail from the painted wall of a villa from Boscoreale; courtesy, Metropolitan Museum of Art; Rogers Fund, 1903)*

PLATE 93: "Still Life with Candy," by Leon van der Hamen; Spanish, 1596–1632. One can imagine the size of a charger that holds twenty such boxes, as served at the feast in St. George's Hall in 1667. *(Museum of Fine Arts, Boston)*

PLATE 94: Sugar temple with cupid. This piece was made by a modern confectioner for the wedding of the daughter of a well-known collector of Wedgwood. Real Wedgwood cameo medallions ornament the dome of the temple which is surrounded with flowers in little vases as seen in the 18th-century engraving by Moreau le Jeune (see Plate 97). Grapes en chemise sparkle on the Wedgwood green glaze plates, and lovely figurines of old Vienna porcelain add charm. *(Wedgwood and all accessories from the Gorely Collection, courtesy of Mr. and Mrs. Charles P. Gorely, Jr; table setting made by the author; photograph by Zitso Studio)*

PLATE 95: Pineapple atop a fruit pyramid, as seen in an 18th-century engraving. The porcelain bowl is on a Sheffield silver dish-cross, setting the pineapple still higher for added drama. *(Arrangement by the author; photograph by George M. Cushing)*

PLATE 96: Fruit pyramid with pineapple on oval platter of Wedgwood's shell ware. The fruit is further dramatized by groups of real shells and by the sweetmeat dish made of real shells to simulate porcelain shell-shaped dishes of the period. A game of true or false could be played here! Eighteenth-century curiosos collected and studied shells and would have been amused by this deception. *(Wedgwood and accessories of the period from the Gorely Collection, courtesy of Mr. and Mrs. Charles P. Gorely, Jr.; sweetmeat dish and arrangement by the author; photograph by Zitso Studio)*

PLATE 97: "Le Souper Fin," by Moreau le Jeune. The pineapple is held by the Three Graces to ornament an intimate supper table in the 18th century. Note the little phials of flowers and tiny artificial trees attached to the plateau. *(Print Department, Museum of Fine Arts, Boston)*

PLATE 98: Compote of mixed fruits and other ornaments for the dessert. This frontispiece is from Beeton's book of household management, 1861. The strawberry plant in a pot was also a favorite idea in the 18th century. *(Courtesy, New York Public Library)*

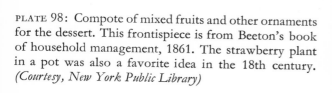

PLATE 99: Chinese woodcut, a bowl of fruit; 17th century.
(Courtesy, Trustees of the British Museum, London)

✹ NINE

Table Appointments to Delight the Eye

THE DINING table has always been a little like a stage for which a scenic designer can conjure up whatever mood or general atmosphere is demanded for a specific occasion. At night, lighted by candles or spotlighted by an overhead chandelier or lamp, it is indeed isolated from the surrounding room as a stage is isolated from a darkened auditorium. In this little island of light, the table setting can even depart, if so desired for a particular reason, from the room's daytime associations of period, color, or design.

Setting a table with imagination and verve can become a beguiling hobby which teams well with a talent for arranging flowers or an interest in collecting antiques or both. Many a hostess develops a collector's flair for assembling interesting table appointments for parties she is likely to give whether formal or informal, and often a centerpiece idea will instigate a search for a whole table "wardrobe" to go with it (Plate 100). Each course may provide a pleasant variation of color and pattern, but there will be sufficient coordination from one to another to carry out a consistent theme throughout the meal.

The possessor of a Chinese Export porcelain basket will haunt antique shops for matching plates or for unusual pieces in similar ware of harmonizing color and design—old "bone" dishes, so useful for salad or corn on the cob, syllabub cups for clear soup or *petits-pots-de-crème,* or leaf-shaped plates for jelly or for the hors d'œuvre. Rummage sales and junk shops sometimes contribute surprising treasures for informal schemes, and who knows what conversation piece

185

may be unearthed for the center of the table demanding just the right linens and other accessories to make it fully effective. The centerpiece may even suggest what food to serve or vice versa, which indicates that many a gourmet with a sense of design may also enjoy this fascinating pursuit.

An antique Chinese earthenware tureen in the shape of a fish was once used as centerpiece at a luncheon in Colorado Springs. Filled with exotic foliage, cleverly selected to suggest aquatic plants which trailed down the table like a long swishy tail, it was much admired as the guests took their seats. But the real proof of imagination and a sense of "theater" came when the main course appeared on lovely celadon plates, each one a perfect foil for the speckled beauty and delectably crisp brown of that delicious regional specialty, a Rocky Mountain trout! To coordinate the decorative quality of food with a perfect setting is the real test of genius in the art of table decoration.

As we examine the table appointments of past centuries, we realize that craftsmen of other days were fully aware of the dramatic possibilities for enhancing the presentation of food by providing beautiful cups, dishes, and other utensils which were not only consistent with the prevailing fashion but were imbued with the individual approach of the designer and the individual demands of a particular patron. These qualities were also present in those objects for the table which were made purely for entertainment, decoration, or display. Not only were these ornaments beautiful in themselves but also much thought was given to their coordination with other appointments and to their effective disposition on the table. It was as if the artists well knew that here was the place, above all others, for detail and perfection of craftsmanship to be appreciated at close range.

The owner of these lovely things also was aware that he had a "captive audience" which could not help noticing his choicest treasures thus set forth on this little "stage," the dining room table. Robert Roberts, butler to Governor Gore of Massachusetts in the early 19th century, probably expressed the point of view of every host or hostess from the time of the ancients through the 19th century when he wrote in his *House Servant's Directory* in 1828, " . . . ladies and gentlemen that have splendid and costly articles wish them to be seen and set out to advantage."

Today it is not so much a question of the display of "splendid and costly articles" as a display of discrimination in the matter of their selection and arrangement. We may deplore mass production and the general "leveling off" of society in the 20th century, but thanks to the incredible variety of attractive wares now available, our table appointments no longer have to be expensive to be worthy of being "seen and set out to advantage." We can take pleasure in the "staging" of the simplest party.

It is true that to choose from such a vast market requires judgment and discernment. The very profusion of possibilities is bewildering, and there is much that is trashy and spurious. Moreover, price is not necessarily a criterion of value. The best way to acquire a trained eye for quality of design, whether in reproductions of traditional forms or in modern inventions, is to study wherever available the beautiful table appointments of other days which were not mass produced but were works of art created by the finest craftsmen for the favored few. To know them and to learn to associate them with their original background is to provide oneself with a standard by which to measure quality in any design, including modern.

Within the narrow compass of a single chapter it is not possible to give anything but the briefest survey of what the past has to offer for our consideration. One can only attempt to give a sense of period by showing a few characteristic examples of each era with, wherever possible, one or two table scenes to suggest the background for which these objects were made. The ideas for centerpieces which have been found to recur periodically in the preceding chapters, have had many interpretations. We shall see that designs for table appointments have also repeated themselves, with changes to suit prevailing fashions, over and over again from earliest times. It may be helpful to trace some of the sources of these designs and to make some interesting comparisons with modern versions.

Ideas from Ancient Egypt

It is unlikely that a flower-show schedule or even a stage setting for amateur theatricals would require the reproduction of an Egyptian table, and it is obvious that an authentic one would be impossible, as artifacts of the period are seldom found outside a major museum. Moreover, in spite of the enormous amount of scholarly research on the subject during the past century, Egyptologists admit that surprisingly little is known of such details of everyday life in ancient Egypt. Ancient Egyptians, alas, did not write books on household management!

But from wall paintings and reliefs of banquet scenes and ceremonial offerings, it appears that the presentation of food was orderly and stylized and that the Egyptians invented the buffet supper, as food was brought to the guests from heaped tables or stands. Bowls of lotus or exotic foliage were often placed amid food, and single blossoms or necklaces of flowers were handed to each guest by slaves. The containers used, whether for flowers or food, were simple yet sophisticated in shape. Many modern containers are their close counterparts (Plate 101), and interesting ideas for modern tables may be gleaned from a study of Egyptian art.

Looking at the ceremonial offerings depicted on the wall of the tomb of Per-Neb, now in the Metropolitan Museum of Art in New York, we feel that anyone with an interest in modern design would covet the low streamlined table with its two egg-shaped casseroles of yellow and blue, smartly banded with black-and-white checks. The triangular blue bowl of lotus on a high narrow base, holding stiffly alternated blossoms, buds, and leaves, also looks modern, and the stands heaped with bread and vegetables are not unlike those used today to display cakes in bakery shop windows. Similar stands of clear glass made in graduated sizes, are sold today to make attractive containers for pyramids of fruit by way of centerpiece. Used *en pyramide* they would be appropriate for a traditional setting, as they are similar to glass centerpieces made in the 18th century. For an Egyptian effect, one large one could be used, painted and then sanded lightly when wet to achieve a texture like pottery, with fruits or vegetables arranged in a squarish mound as seen in Plates 103 and 104.

In this day of individuality a hostess is certainly not committed to any one style for inspiration in selecting her table appointments. She can adapt ideas from various sources which seem in character with her own house and with a specific occasion. For example, an outdoor meal in a modern setting might be a routine sort of picnic with the casual charm of crude pottery and wooden bowls. Or it could be lavishly exotic in the Hawaiian manner, which is not unlike an Egyptian banquet. Either food or flowers may be set forth in an ancient Polynesian poi bowl; fruit or the hors d'œuvre might be served in a long leaf-shaped dish of wood or in a coconut spathe; or a choice of hot mustard or pepper sauce for each guest could be presented in the two outspread wings of a white china butterfly, a modern version of the age-old use of forms from nature in ceramics for tableware (Plate 102). Hawaiians follow the Egyptian custom of garnishing a dish of fruit with a single exotic blossom, perhaps a lotus, an orchid, or a spray of fragrant ginger (*Zingiber officinale*), a touch which would be equally charming today. Any of these ideas are in the modern spirit or, for that matter, in the spirit of the Egyptians.

The Heritage of Greece and Rome

Greek and Roman table appointments also have an affinity for modern design (Plate 105), and reproductions of Greek and Etruscan vases in a dull-finished black composition resembling pottery are much favored today as containers for fruit or flowers. Wedgwood in the 18th century made bowls and other tableware of black basalt in classic Greek and Roman shapes, and the Wedgwood factory is still making them, fully aware of their stylish appearance in a modern setting. Originally introduced during the Classic Revival, they are, of course, equally at home in a late 18th- or early 19th-century dining room.

An example of Roman cameo glass of the 1st century A.D. in Plate 106 shows clearly the exquisite perfection of design and craftsmanship achieved at the height of the Roman Empire. (Plate 107, derived from Roman examples, is a distinctly modern interpretation of this ancient technique.) A 3rd-century silver fruit dish in the shape of a shell is the forerunner of a long line of shell dessert dishes (Fig. 8), to this day a favorite form not only in silver but also in ceramic and glass. The fluted silver bowl of the same period appears often in the 18th century with the same general aspect and continues to be reproduced today (Plate 109). A glass flask in the shape of a fish, made in the 3rd century (Plate 110) is an example of the fanciful use of animal, bird, or fish forms for vessels to hold liquids. Countless interpretations of this same idea are to be found throughout the centuries in all sorts of materials. These are, no doubt, a reflection of the very human love of a "conversation piece" and today's versions satisfy the same desire. (See Plates 108, 111, and the straw swan illustrated in Plate 12.)

Ancient Greek unglazed or partially glazed kitchen or storage pots bear an amazing resemblance to French earthenware casseroles and frying pans today. We may smile, indeed, as we read in a little pamphlet called *Pots and Pans of Classical Athens,* that the Greek poet Euboulus said of those of his own day:

> "Grinning up at me
> The casserole boils and chatters to itself
> And fishes leap up in the frying pans."

These simple utensils are so familiar that it is not difficult, in spite of the intervening centuries, to get a picture of warmth, unpretentious comfort, and casual charm that might be duplicated in any kitchen or family room today.

Details of Roman usage are more available than those of Greece, and a greater variety of Roman artifacts have survived. Francis Henry Taylor in *The Taste*

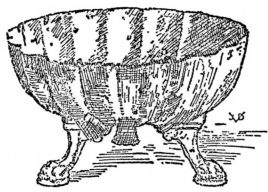

FIGURE 8: Roman fruit dishes, 3rd century. These are in shell and fluted shapes often seen in 18th-century silver. *(Drawings from* Apicius, *a cookbook of the 3rd century, edited by J. D. Vehling; Chicago, 1936)*

of Angels tells us that at a banquet given by Trimalchio, a Roman parvenu, "a donkey of Corinthian bronze stood on the sideboard, with panniers holding olives, white on one side, black on the other." The donkey, with his panniers, is a well-known friend! Pottery donkeys with baskets for olives or condiments still abound in peasant wares from Italy, Mexico, and Spain, and the idea even occasionally appears in a grander version. A pair of silver-gilt donkeys with panniers for salt and pepper, made by Garrard for the Great Exhibition at the Crystal Palace in London in 1851, may be seen today on the table in the State dining room at Longleat, country house of the Marquis of Bath.

Trimalchio's banquet, Taylor says, also boasted "sausages laid on a silver grill [or grid] with damsons and seeds of pomegranates under it." This serving piece has had countless descendants through the centuries. As it was the custom in ancient times to have most of the cooking done close to the table, much care was lavished on the design of the equipment and on the containers in which hot food was placed for serving. The idea repeats itself today; handsomely designed grills are now offered for the barbeque terrace and some of them have a classic simplicity. A recently translated and published cookbook by one Apicius, of whom nothing is known except that his book is an authentic document of Imperial Roman days, shows illustrations of equipment of this kind now in the National Museum at Naples. In the collection are two wonderful examples of the *thermospodium*, an early version of the chafing dish. This was a charcoal-burning heater for the service of hot foods in the dining room. Not only utilitarian but extremely good looking, these examples have beautiful sphinx feet, lion-head handles, and other classic ornamental details (Plate 112 and Fig. 9).

The chafing dish, or *réchaud*, appears frequently thereafter, with interesting examples found in the 17th, 18th, and early 19th centuries, becoming more and more classic in derivation. Another utensil used for cooking on the table in the early 19th century is the egg-cooker, a metal container on feet, fitted with a rack

FIGURE 9: A Roman thermospodium of plain design; water and food heater for everyday purposes. Charcoal fuel was used. Foods were kept on the top area in pans, dishes or pots, and were thus carried from the kitchen into the dining room. (Apicius. *The drawings from this book are from original Roman examples in the National Museum, Naples*)

to hold the eggs which are coddled by pouring boiling water over them and keeping them tightly covered until done. Incidentally, no better way of getting a satisfactory soft-boiled egg has ever been found. Some egg-cookers have claw feet, lion-head handles, and other detail borrowed from the Roman *thermo-spodium* (Plate 113).

Many of us have antique table appointments with classic detail, treasures either inherited or still collectible. We find them not only appropriate for a Georgian or Federal background but also readily adaptable to a modern setting of sophisticated design. It is rewarding to study, in museums and in today's marvelously illustrated books and museum catalogues, the sources from which they are derived.

The Dark Ages

The decline of the Roman Empire in the 5th century greatly diminished the market for rich table appointments. Due to invasions and political unrest, many workshops making fine silver or cameo glass had to close down and skilled craftsmen were forced to turn to making simpler, utilitarian ware. Many glass vessels of this kind made in the Frankish and Merovingian period (4th to 8th century) have survived (Plate 114) and that this type of glassware was still in use in the Middle Ages is seen in the 13th-century Italian fresco of the Last Supper (Plate 115). Here we see many shapes that have come down to the present day, familiar to us in silver, ceramic, and glass. It would be difficult to improve upon them.

The tablecloth in this fresco is most interesting because of the decorative *longière,* a separate strip of linen hung in festoons along the side of the table over another cloth of a darker color. The *longière,* according to medieval custom, served in place of napkins for the guests. Lacking forks, everyone ate with his fingers, and when the great basins and ewers were passed several times during a meal, the *longière* was conveniently available. When forks[1] came into fashion (in the 17th century in Italy and rarely before the 18th century elsewhere on the Continent and in England), napkins also appeared and the hand-washing at table had merely a token survival in the form of the finger bowl.

The *longière* in this particular fresco seems to be attached to the under cloth by means of tapes hung on buttons or pegs, and its handsome borders, similar to but not exactly matching the borders on the cloth itself, make it a decorative feature as well as a useful one.

Though no strewn flowers are shown on this table, this was a period when they were most certainly used. The round objects probably represent the customary individual loaves of bread to be cut in half to serve as "trenchers," and though the artist did not trouble to paint them in much detail, he did lavish considerable precision on the drawing of the tall pitchers, the cups, beakers, and ornamental dishes for the fish, as well as on the meticulously rendered detail of the tablecloth.

The Middle Ages

A table scene which will serve to represent the late Middle Ages is found in a detail from a Flemish tapestry of the 15th century known as the Esther Tapestry (Plate 116). Queen Esther, though a Biblical character, is naïvely pictured in medieval dress, sitting at a royal medieval table. We can see that she is a queen, not only because of her crown (and a rather extraordinary one it is, three tiers high and tied on under her chin!) but also because she possesses a splendid nef, the rich ornament on wheels which vaguely suggests the shape of a ship and which was a table ornament permitted only to royalty. She also has a gold *hanap* or covered, footed cup, some beautiful knives of ebony and ivory inlaid with silver, and a small cup of Venetian glass, something very new and luxurious at that time indeed.

The tablecloth is of fine damask in a lozenge pattern. Damask was so-called because from the 12th century it was most beautifully woven in Damascus and was one of the most sumptuous fabrics of the Middle Ages. Silver platters gleam resplendently, but the simple little square plate before her, known as a "trencher," is of wood. It seems crude in contrast to the rest of the appointments, but it served the humble purpose of providing a practical surface on which meat could be cut into manageable pieces to be eaten with the fingers, for as we have said, forks were not used for meat at this time.

Even earlier than the 15th century, royal table appointments might have been richly ornamented with jewels or colorful enamels, or intricately fashioned of silver or silver gilt with figures of men, animals, birds, or twining foliage. However, in contrast to the delicacy and grace of such naturalistic detail, there was also an element of solidity and generous scale which made every work of art of the period a happy marriage of masculine strength and feminine charm.

Of course not every table in the Middle Ages was so splendidly adorned.

Less important households used sturdy and utilitarian ware of pottery, pewter, or wood, and the general aspect of common cups, bowls, and pitchers did not change as much with passing fashions as did those on the Grand Table. The kitchenware shown even in some 17th-century paintings is almost the same sort of ware that would have been found on much earlier tables. It is the kind of simple equipment that might have been accorded to medieval varlets who sat "below the salt" at a great lord's feast and who sometimes on a pilgrimage, when there was not room to seat all retainers in the village inn, sat at trestle tables in the street where "candles set in blossoming pear trees assisted the moon to light the scene."

For an alfresco party in this mood today, there is a wealth of simple and attractive pottery or woodenware from which to choose. A large pitcher of modern pottery in Plate 117 shows the characteristic medieval pinched spout, subtle shape, and primitive type of ornamentation found in medieval examples. It is a warm olive brown, rough in texture, and worthy of masquerading as a medieval accessory at the flower show or in a stage setting for a Shakespearean play, as well as being a handsome container for autumn foliage or roadside flowers in a pine room or on a modern terrace.

Oddly enough, the medieval spirit is often found in the ultramodern house today—the "natural house" as Frank Lloyd Wright called it, the sort of house which at first seems starkly simple but which looks out through vast areas of thermo-glass into a pine wood or the intricacies of a grove of white birches, or lacking this opportunity for a touch of nature, perhaps brings the out-of-doors inside with shrubs planted in pockets of earth set in a flagstone floor. Here is a setting where naturalistic detail may be found in an imaginative use of driftwood, in free-form pottery bowls, or in designs from nature printed on rough linens or woven into a woolen fabric. Simple motifs, perhaps of a single acorn and oak leaf or a culinary herb block-printed or embroidered on table linens remind one of individual plant forms in the background of a *millefleur* tapestry.

Modern glassmakers offer heavy glass goblets of a shape often seen on medieval tables. Outsized ones, intended for vases, can be used as hurricane shields for candles (Plate 76). Modern enameled glass recalls the deep glowing colors of medieval enamels. Glass or pottery oil-and-vinegar cruets are made today in a two-way fashion that goes back to the 15th century, and pottery goblets with a very modern look are copied from Renaissance examples in the shape of fat pine cones (Plate 118). The modern hostess in her "natural house" can have her informality in the grand manner of the seigneur, if she likes, or she can create an atmosphere of rough-hewn simplicity like that of the duke's retainers.

As for color and texture on a table inspired by the Middle Ages, if authenticity is not required, one can suggest the love of gold seen in medieval manuscript illuminations by using a tablecloth of saffron yellow, perhaps even of burlap to suggest the rough surface of a Gothic tapestry. With it, bright linen napkins in several hues—clear blue, vermilion, blue-green, and green, a color scheme straight out of an Italian primitive—would be effective.

To be authentic, of course, a medieval cloth would be white, of the finest linen damask, perhaps laid over a darker cloth and with a *longière* hung along the side. But an independent table could use a soft range of colors taken from tapestries or, in a lighter key, from the muted frescoes of Giotto or Fra Angelico, subtly mellowed and dimmed by time, with warm grays, analogous reds, pale lavender, and burnt orange opposed by almond green and the wonderful faded primary blue. Like a unifying thread through all these colors would run the inevitable medieval gold, not a tinsely sort of gold but one with the richness of beaten gold or of gold leaf laid over a foundation of green or vermilion. For a challenging study of how to use the entire spectrum in a single composition, there are no better examples than in Italian frescoes of the 14th and 15th centuries.

During our Western Middle Ages, the Orient tells a different story and may offer inspiration for a modern house where an exotic flavor is wanted. In China table appointments for a "literary gathering" were much more sophisticated in the 12th century than those set for royalty in the Esther Tapestry three centuries later. In the Chinese scene shown in Plate 119 where servants are busy at side tables, notice the grace and refinement of the tall ewers or wine pots and the delicate porcelain bowls with their black lacquer stands. The shapes of some of the other jars and dishes were copied much later in European porcelain of the 18th century, as were those of the porcelain ladles. There is a lovely great covered basket and a decorative little "safe" to keep food protected from dust and insects, and there are two beautiful bronze braziers and a huge tank with water to keep the wine cool.

See also, in Plate 120, a Korean cup-stand of the Koryo period (918–1392), its tray shaped like gently overlapping flower petals, a simple yet sophisticated piece which might be, and often is, duplicated today for a modern cocktail buffet. Flower and plant forms have always been charmingly used in Oriental ceramics. A wine pot of Korean celadon has the shape of a gourd, with the handle in the form of a twisted lotus stem, and another, also of the 12th century, has its cover in the shape of a bamboo sprout. A lovely Chinese teapot of the Ming period (1368–1643) is of stoneware, its surface slightly puckered to represent "a brown pear skin." There is nothing crude about the Oriental ceramics of the Middle Ages. They were so elegant that they were copied delightedly in that age of elegance, the 18th century (Plate 121).

The Renaissance

One aspect of the Renaissance particularly relevant to our subject is the increased development of the arts which flourished in a new climate of artistic awakening and creativity, not only in Italy where the movement had its richest manifestation but also in varying degrees all over Europe. Especially in the affluent society of the Netherlands in the 15th and 16th centuries was there a growing luxury among the nobility and also among wealthy bankers and merchants who could afford fine establishments and sumptuous table appointments.

In a detail from Jan Brueghel's painting "The Sense of Taste" we see a fine lady enjoying a banquet of rare delicacies at a table adorned with splendid appointments of the period. Jan ("Velvet") Brueghel (1568–1625) loved to paint still life, and here he has omitted no detail of the elegant Flemish table of the late Renaissance (Plate 122). In addition to the spectacular peacock pie and other game-bird pies adorned with their own plumage, we see on this table a lovely footed salver, perhaps of silver gilt, holding fruit. There is also a tall goblet either of Venetian glass or of the almost equally beautiful glass *façon de Venise* which was by this time made in the Low Countries in skillful imitation. Behind one of the bird pies we glimpse a "pillar salt" which may have been either of silver or earthenware, and lobsters sprawl on a handsome delft plate. The tablecloth still provides a *longière* in place of a napkin, a fashion soon to be out of date, but the lady's most unusual and avant-garde piece of equipment is the little three-tined fork with which she is eating oysters. At this time forks were considered a ridiculous and rather effeminate fashion, but apparently they were used for oysters and sticky preserved fruits some time before they were adopted for meats. Scribner's *Dictionary of Antiques and the Decorative Arts* (1957) says that in English silver a little two-tined fork with a spoon on the other end was called a "sucket fork" and was used for sweetmeats during the Tudor

PLATE 100: A table wardrobe of 19th-century ware. Oriental influence in pleasant variety of color and scale sets the theme throughout the meal and can be used in effective contrast with plain ware of the same period such as grandmother's prized Limoges. Note curved bone dish, Canton whale ramekin, and covered syllabub cup—all of which have various uses. Simple soup bowl from San Francisco's Chinatown looks handsome on antique Japanese Imari patterned plate. *(From the author's collection; photograph by Francis Lambert)*

PLATE 101: A modern Japanese lacquer stand similar to those seen in Egyptian wall paintings. The low oval dish which looks ancient was purchased recently in Taos, New Mexico. The book displayed is *Egyptian Wall Paintings from Tombs and Temples*, UNESCO. *(Photograph by Francis Lambert)*

PLATE 102: White china butterfly. Made today in Japan, this dish is used in a South Pacific restaurant for individual service of two kinds of sauce. *(Photograph by Francis Lambert)*

PLATE 103: Egyptian bowl of lotus amid food; 2560–2420 B.C. A highly stylized arrangement of lotus in a footed bowl between stands laden with fruit and other produce. Note modern effect not only of flower arrangement but of the low table and interesting casseroles. *(From reconstruction of the tomb of Per-Neb; Metropolitan Museum of Art, New York)*

PLATE 104: King Rameses I bringing garlanded offering to Isis and Osiris; *c.* 1315 B.C. While these offerings of fruit and other produce would not be copied literally, there is a very striking and dramatic design in the shape of the squarish mounds and in the decorative contrast of large and small forms which might suggest an idea for a fruit arrangement in a modern setting. This is a detail of a limestone wall relief from the Temple of Abydos. *(Metropolitan Museum of Art, New York; gift of J. Pierpont Morgan, 1911)*

PLATE 105: Group of black wares. Included are two pieces of Wedgwood's black basaltes: one, a 19th-century vase with rococo influence in the shape but having classic detail of cupid with a garland; the other, a large bowl made by Wedgwood today. The two vases on the right are museum reproductions of Greek shapes, a tall stem-cup and a low cantharus. The book, *Greek Painting,* by Pierre Devanbez is opened here to show a stunning kylix from Chios and the pattern on the inside of a Laconian cup. *(Photograph by Francis Lambert)*

PLATE 106: Roman cameo glass cup of the 1st century. Cameo glass was made by covering a foundation of colored glass with a layer of translucent white glass which was then carved with ornamental designs illustrating mythological and other subjects. *(Corning Museum of Glass, New York)*

PLATE 107: Engraved glass cup by Edward Hald; Orrefors glass, 1920. The figures, apparently projecting, are in reality deeply hollowed in a technique similar to that of the Roman intaglio. The design is also classic (as Plate 106) yet unmistakably modern in spirit. *(Nationalmuseum, Stockholm)*

PLATE 108: Table vessels in animal forms. The three examples show an owl, early 17th century, German (facing page); a cow, 18th century, of English delft (facing page); cow cream-and-sugar set, Vermont pottery, 1964. *(German owl and English delft cow, Museum of Fine Arts, Boston; photograph of Vermont pottery set by Francis Lambert)*

PLATE 109: Irish Georgian silver bowl showing Roman influence. *(Museum of Fine Arts, Boston)*

PLATE 110: Flask in the form of a fish; Roman Empire, probably Syria, 3rd century. *(Corning Museum of Glass, New York)*

PLATE 111: Ancient pottery bull from N. W. Iran, *c.* 1000–880 B.C. This is an early example of an animal form used for pouring liquids. One might almost believe it to be modern pottery. *(Museum of Fine Arts, Boston)*

PLATE 112: Elaborate Roman thermospodium, heater for the service of hot foods and drinks in the dining room. The fuel was charcoal. This specimen was found at Stabix, one of the ill-fated towns destroyed by the eruption of Mt. Vesuvius. *(Photograph from* Apicius, *edited by J.D. Vehling, Chicago, 1936)*

PLATE 113: Classic shapes. This group of egg-cookers in Sheffield silver, tin, and brass shows that classic forms were still popular in the 19th century. The brass one (right) is egg-shaped when the cover is on, and holds three eggs in the removable rack inside. In the other examples, notice typical Roman fluting, beading, lion-head handles, and acanthus leaf detail (on handles of the racks). *(From author's collection; photograph by Francis Lambert)*

PLATE 114: Frankish glass, 4th to 7th centuries. The glass, in conical shape, is similar in color and texture to modern Mexican glass. *(Metropolitan Museum of Art, New York; gift of J. Pierpont Morgan, 1917)*

PLATE 115: Italian fresco of the Last Supper, late 13th century. Note the extra strip of tablecloth hung in festoons, used in place of napkins, and the Roman shapes in glass and earthenware table appointments. *(Worcester Art Museum)*

PLATE 116: The Esther Tapestry; Flemish, *c.* 1475. *(Minneapolis Museum of Arts)*

PLATE 117: A modern pitcher reminiscent of medieval contours and ornamentation. *(Photograph by Francis Lambert)*

PLATE 118: Italian Majolica cup in the shape of a pine cone; from Gubbio, *c.* 1520. Similar pottery cups are made in Italy today. *(Museum of Fine Arts, Boston)*

PLATE 119: Oriental table appointments on serving tables, 12th century. This group is in the foreground of a Chinese painting on silk. It represents a literary gathering having refreshments in the garden (also see Plate 53). *(Collections of the National Palace and Central Museums, Taiwan)*

PLATE 120: Flower-shaped cup-stand of Korean celadon; 918–1392. This is a simple table appointment which would be useful and attractive today in either a traditional or a modern setting. Oriental pottery was often inspired by forms in nature as it still is today (white china butterfly from Japan, Plate 102). *(Cup-stand, courtesy of Museum of Fine Arts, Boston)*

PLATE 121: Early Wedgwood creamware and pearl ware in leaf and vegetable shapes. *(Courtesy, Jean Gorely, secretary of the Wedgwood Club, Boston)*

PLATE 122: "The Sense of Taste," by Jan ("Velvet") Brueghel; Flemish, 1585–1625, part of a series called "The Allegory of The Senses." Detail shows fruit in a tall compote and several game pies ornamented with the bird's own plumage, decoration enough for this lavish table. Note pillar salt and stemmed goblet of Venetian glass. The lady is using an oyster fork, a luxury at the time. *(Prado, Madrid)*

PLATE 123: Venetian glass ewer, late 15th century. The enameled medallion shows a lady holding a Venetian glass goblet. *(Cleveland Museum of Art; purchase from the J. H. Wade Fund)*

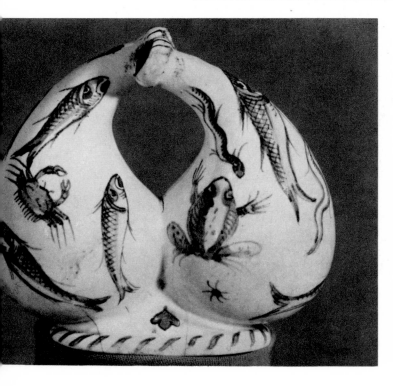

PLATE 126: English silver pillar salt; London, 1580–1600. Salt was a costly but indispensable commodity and was regarded with veneration. It was even considered a safeguard against witchcraft. Consequently, on the Grand Table in the Middle Ages and during the Renaissance elaborate containers were made for it, and it assumed a position of importance on the table comparable to that of the nef in France. *(Museum of Fine Arts, Boston)*

PLATE 127: Table ornament of St. Porchaire faïence, 16th century. Perhaps this French piece was used for flowers or sweetmeats on sticks. *(Cleveland Museum of Art; purchase from the J. H. Wade Fund)*

PLATE 128: Engraving, expressing the exuberance and fanfare of a 17th-century party. *(From the title page of* Les Plaisirs de l'Isle Enchantée; *courtesy, Harvard College Library)*

PLATE 129: Baroque buffet. An elaborate buffet, built around the courtyard fountain in the Cour de Marbre, Versailles, shows garlands and high pyramids of fruit, with candles and torches spiraling in a column of light reaching to the top of the Palace. *(Engraving by Lepautre from* Les Divertissemens de Versailles *by André Félibien, Paris, 1676; courtesy, Harvard College Library)*

period. For oysters it would seem that a similar utensil would be not only practical but indispensable. Mrs. Stone, in *Chronicles of Fashion,* says that Queen Elizabeth I possessed several forks which had been presented to her but that they were not used since forks did not come into fashion until much later. However, these gifts might well have been "sucket forks" as the description of their delicate elegance would indicate. One of them was, according to an inventory in Nichols' *Progresses of Queen Elizabeth* (Mrs. Stone's source of information), of "christall," garnished with gold and "sparcks of garnetts" and the others were of gold, ornamented with jewels and a "lytle corall." Such exquisite table appointments the fastidious Queen Elizabeth would have enjoyed using, either for oysters or sweetmeats one might imagine.

For examples of existing table appointments of this period we show a magnificent enameled Venetian glass ewer of the 15th century (Plate 123), an English pillar salt (Plate 126), a cruet of the now very rare Medici porcelain (Plate 125), and an extraordinary ornament of French St. Porchaire faïence (Plate 127), perhaps made to hold salt at the top and with part of its base perforated for flowers or sweetmeats on sticks. If flowers were used in this they would have been artificial as there is apparently no way to get any water inside.

All of these examples are in museums and comparable ones are unlikely to be available even in reproduction. Except for the amusing little oil-and-vinegar cruet, which does appear frequently in a modern version, they seem out of character with our contemporary tables, but they are all indicative of the richness and grandeur of the Renaissance and evoke an era of great luxury and marvelous craftsmanship.

Richness of color and texture, also, were typical of the Renaissance. The glowing reds, warm browns, sumptuous golds, sapphire blues, and deep forest greens together with the wonderfully gleaming satins and thick-piled velvets, their folds highlighted by the *chiaroscuro* of the Renaissance painters, give us a vivid picture of the luxurious fashions of the time.

Baroque Splendor and Colonial Fashions in the 17th Century

In Europe the 17th century was an era of swaggering bravado and high style. All was sound and fury, movement, restless agitation. Gone was the restraint and measured, classical cadence of the Renaissance.

Appropriate for this mood was the adoption of the great sweeping S-curve which might almost be called the hallmark of 17th-century design. It seemed to typify the very spirit of the time, this "living line" which contributed drama and flourish to everything from a courtier's plumed hat to the arabesques in Le Nôtre's embroidered parterres in the garden at Versailles. It gave grace to otherwise ponderous furniture; it swirled intricately in the great candelabra and chandeliers; it even embellished with curving volutes the elaborate temporary buffets set up for special festivities around a courtyard fountain or in a garden bosquet (Plate 129). The same vigorous reverse curve, which Hogarth later referred to as the "Line of Beauty," formed the underlying structure of many of the Dutch and Flemish flower paintings of the late 17th century. It was a line of enormous vitality and drive.

Curiously enough, almost the only place where the S-curve was not used at this time was in the fruit-and-flower arrangements on the table or on the buffet. These were static and monumental in character, retaining the rigid symmetry of Renaissance design and acting as stabilizing accents amid the tortuous curves of a baroque *surtout-de-table* or of elaborate sugar ornaments, the latter now very large and resembling baroque sculpture. Twisted also were the candelabra, and even the napkins were folded in a fantastic manner to represent shells, swans, or other figures. But some of the table appointments were of a solid grandeur since magnificence was also a key requirement of the day. Occasionally a "curiosity" such as a vessel made from a coconut, an ostrich egg (Plate 132), or a nautilus shell enlivened the scene.

In Dutch and Flemish still-life paintings of the 17th century we find a wealth of specific examples of table appointments, although they are assembled as the painter wished to place them and not as they would have appeared on the table. Such extraneous details as butterflies, insects, and sprays of currants or strawberries have been added simply because the artist wanted to paint them. Their inclusion reflects the beginning of interest in natural history, and if fruit was depicted as fly specked or leaves riddled with holes, it was a grim symbol of *vanitas,* a pious reminder that all natural beauty was subject to impairment and decay.

The Dutch artist Pieter Claesz paints with consummate skill and realism, characteristic pieces of glass and pewter of the period (Plate 133). And Floris van Schooten, another Dutch painter, spreads before us a handsome display of delft bowls and chargers filled with fruit, with a beautiful porcelain dish on a silver-gilt stand and two magnificent gold-and-silver *hanaps,* or covered cups (Plate 130).

The tablecloths in both paintings are interesting, showing the customary use of a white linen cloth over a dark one of a richer fabric. If anyone possessed an Oriental rug, a treasure considered far too valuable to be used on the floor, it was generally exhibited on the table between meals, then protected by a linen cloth during a meal.

To give a sense of the baroque style, it is rewarding to study typical color harmonies of the period. Seventeenth-century fabrics were thick and luxurious with the subdued, shadowed luster of velvet or heavily ribbed silk; colors were dark and rich if a little gloomy. In his diary for October 19, 1660, Samuel Pepys records with satisfaction that his dining room is "finished with green serge hanging and gilt leather, which is very handsome." Elizabeth Jenkins describes 17th-century colors in dress among other aspects of Jacobean art as having "a strange consistency with the spirit of the age . . . a somber, livid range of colors: in black and dim gold, in gray and lacquer red, in white and deepest crimson; their gems were milky, translucent pearls, black onyx, red carnelian." Perhaps, despite their love of luxury, the warning of *vanitas* was always a specter in the back of their minds.

In America, while 17th-century architecture was necessarily simpler and followed medieval traditions rather than the European baroque style, not everything the colonists used was by any means rough or crude. Of course in the earliest days of colonization wooden trenchers, bowls, and mugs were the general equipment on New England tables, but there was soon a good deal of pewter, silver, and pottery. Most of this was imported from England, but much fine silver was made in the colonies in the 17th century, and wealthy colonists also had delftware from Holland (later copied in England and imported also). Even blue-and-white K'ang-hsi porcelains, brought to England via Holland by the Dutch East India Company, were thence imported to America. Kathryn C. Buhler, authority on American silver, points out that silver was treasured by well-to-do colonists as security in time of trouble, for it could always be melted down "without much loss," as a Virginia colonist expressed it, and turned into ready cash.

Some of the fine possessions which a New England gentleman might have owned are set forth in the 17th-century Boxford Room in the Museum of Fine Arts, Boston (Plate 134). Such valuable pieces of course were usually displayed on the "court cupboard," the important piece of furniture which took the place of the European buffet where such things were kept as in a treasury.

However, in comparison to Europe, there was little opportunity for luxury or entertainment on the European scale. For the most part craftsmen were far too busy supplying the necessities of life to devote time to the production of such frivolities as wine fountains and fanciful sugar ornaments, however much the more affluent colonists might have enjoyed emulating high fashions in aristocratic circles abroad.

Of course persons of consequence had brought with them a few items of luxury. Governor Winslow (1595–1655) of the Plymouth Plantation had a set of twelve "banketting" dishes depicting the twelve months of the year. These, of which only one survives (Plate 135), were of wood, ornamented—on the bottom—with pasted-on engravings accompanied by a verse of "poesy" which was to be read or sung by each guest in turn. This was a custom which must have helped to alleviate some of the grimmer aspects of Puritan austerity. It is cheering to picture Governor Winslow and his guests warming themselves with October ale, singing that "November pulls down hoggs for Bacon, Porke and Souse / Housewife save for puddings, goode meate in poor man's Howse."[2]

Thus a few treasured possessions salvaged from a more abundant life in England were occasionally seen, but the household equipment of the average colonist was simple in the extreme. According to Alice Morse Earle, in *Home Life in Colonial Days,* the dining table of the colonists was "usually a long narrow board . . . with no legs attached. It was laid on supports or trestles shaped like a saw-horse. Thus it was literally a board and was called a 'table board' and the linen cover used . . . was not called a tablecloth but a board cloth or board clothes." Important indeed was the colonist who had a "table dormant," that is, a dining table which remained in place between meals. In *Medieval Panorama,* G. G. Coulton points out that "it was a distinctive note of Chaucer's Franklin's great hospitality that he had a 'table dormant' in his hall," which shows that this custom had been in use since the Middle Ages.

Some of the finest pieces of American silver of this period (and also of pewter, English or Dutch delft, or Chinese porcelain) are now in museums, but many are still found in private collections or are even in actual use by people fortunate enough to have inherited them. Although few examples of American silver of this date, such as the richly ornamented "sugar box" on the table in the Boxford Room, reflect the more elaborate style fashionable in Europe, most of them have a quiet simplicity relying upon subtle shape, faultless proportions, and the lovely patina of the silver itself for distinction. These qualities are much appreciated by collectors today.

Thus far there seems to be no documentary evidence of the use of flowers on the dining table of the American colonists, but since we know that flowers were so used in Europe in the 17th century, there is no reason to suppose that colonists with an aristocratic background did not enjoy the same pleasant custom whenever flowers were available. Cultivated ground was limited since it had to be fenced and was used chiefly for herbs, vegetables, and fruit, but perhaps a colonial housewife would have found pleasure in field flowers and would have arranged them in stiff little bunches in "moss baskets" or in an empty apothecary jar. Fruit pyramids, too, doubtless graced the colonial table.

But the European baroque style as well as the American colonial has a modern appeal, and the drama and flourish of sweeping curves and swelling forms has greatly influenced modern design. For baroque is not so much a period as a state of mind. Anyone with a sense of theater and love of the flamboyant is likely to adopt this style, finding that it relieves the stark aridity of modern interiors which often need to be enlivened with some form of plasticity and rhythmic detail. A solution to this problem sometimes seen in the ultramodern house of a wealthy collector is the combination of abstract paintings with the vigorous sweeping lines of baroque furniture.

Less affluent collectors of modern art catch the same spirit when they haunt junk shops for decorative objects with rhythmic interplay of line—plaster cherubs, huge shells, soda-fountain chairs. These seem to "go" with the most modern tableware which is often grandiose in scale and generous with free-form curves.

In this day of individuality "Modern Baroque," a definite revival in the 20th century, appeals to many, while others with a more quiet taste may prefer that other great revival of our times, "Modern Classic." This third historic revival of the pure Greek and Roman forms of antiquity is as different from the original as it is different from the Renaissance or the Classic Revival of the 18th century. Still others cling to the simple, comfortable design of early American silver, pottery, or pewter. As individualists we are free to choose.

The 18th Century

The 18th century comprised three moods: one of symmetry and Palladian dignity in the first quarter of the century, followed by the exuberant gaiety and cap-over-the-mill asymmetry of the rococo, returning abruptly in the last quarter of the century to a new sort of classic dignity derived from original Greek and Roman sources. But in spite of these differences, there was one thing shared by all three 18th-century styles—the love of a gleaming surface.

This new quality began quietly enough in the early 18th century and in England was only noticeable because even a soft gleam of lightness was in such sharp contrast to the somber dark colors and textures that had been fashionable during the reign of William and Mary. Light-colored silks and satins replaced heavy, dull-finished fabrics, and the simple, almost unornamented surfaces of Queen Anne silver reflected more light than had the ornately chased and elaborately *repoussé* silver of the 17th century. In England there was also an increased importation of Oriental porcelain which perhaps set the key for lighter forms, subtle curves, more delicate colors, and the desire for light-reflecting qualities in other aspects of the decorative arts.

In Germany, early in the century, there was a more sudden transition to the cult of lightness. The excitement of the new European porcelain (a formula long sought throughout Europe and at last achieved at Meissen, near Dresden in 1709), was exhilarating, and designers exploited its marvelous translucency in a new way, manipulating it in deep sweeping curves which reflected light with flashing brilliance.

England had to wait until almost mid-century before this new porcelain was available to any but the very wealthy, but meanwhile there was happiness enough in the possession of the Oriental porcelain so long coveted and now more readily obtainable (though still expensive). With the porcelain from the Orient came tea, also a luxury but not as prohibitive in price as it had been in the 17th century, and the sudden fashion for tea-drinking called for a whole new type of equipment such as tea bowls, kettles, and tea caddies, none of which had existed before in English silver. We can see some of these new and elegant appointments proudly displayed in "A British Family at Tea," an early 18th-century painting by an unknown artist (Plate 136). That it is a very new fashion indeed to drink tea is obvious from the uncertainty of each member of the family as to the proper way to hold the delicate little handleless porcelain cups.

Since the tea came from the Orient, it is natural that the shapes of teapots and other requirements for the tea service would be adopted by English silversmiths from the shapes already known for these objects in Chinese porcelain which were suavely simple and gently curving, often based on naturalistic forms. There was an occasional touch of Palladian classicism as in the fluted bowls, but the shapes derived from Chinese porcelain, particularly the pear shape of the teakettle and its swan-necked spout, now greatly influenced English silver and, later, English porcelain until the last quarter of the century when the classic designs of Robert Adam prevailed.

In the rococo period, in mid-century, the love of "glister" and *givrage,* a frostlike sparkle, became an obsession not only in silver but in everything else on the table. It was achieved by fair means or foul, from the shining elegance of the new porcelain (Plates 137 and 138), the bright mirror plateaux, and crystal candelabra or chandeliers, to the artificial glitter provided by frosting grapes or flowers with sugar or coating sugar ornaments with powdered glass, making them "shine like the eye of a cat." During the Classic Revival the quality of brilliance was achieved by more sophisticated and less obvious means, such as increased sparkle and perfection in crystal devices to reflect candlelight (Plate 140) and the new method of bright-cut engraving on silver, a series of small, deeply incised geometrical shapes or zigzag lines which added to an effect of brilliance.

Another irresistible persuasion of fashion which was consistently admired throughout the 18th century, even invading the most sacred halls of classicism, was the vogue for chinoiserie. The arresting strangeness of the mysterious East never failed to capture the imagination of a theater-loving society which seemed to accept the Orient as a dream world of fantasy, and however vague or wildly imaginative European ideas of the Orient might be, they had an enormous appeal. Chinese railings enclosed the garden-parterre centerpiece even though there might be a Greek temple in the middle, Chinese "images" were made of porcelain or sugar, epergnes turned into Oriental pagodas, and parties were given in what was fondly imagined to be "the Chinese manner" (Plate 141).

Robert Adam alone seems to have been disturbed when one of his classic dining rooms was invaded by chinoiserie or by rococo silver, as often happened. Toward the end of the century he himself designed appropriately classic table appointments (Plate 142) and furniture for customers who wanted their furnishings in "the purest taste," and other designers of silver and porcelain eventually followed suit.

There was a fascinating exhibit staged in several of the period rooms in the Metropolitan Museum of Art in New York in 1964—"reoccupying them in style" by figures in costumes of the period from the Museum's Costume Institute. It was interesting to see a Chippendale chair with chinoiserie motifs and a very rococo candelabrum by Paul de Lamerie in the severely classic dining room from Lansdowne House by Robert Adam (Plate 143). By 1790 fashions in dress as well as table appointments would have caught up with the classic mood, and Mr. Adam would have been pleased to see the ladies wearing straight, high-waisted dresses in the "antique" or "Grecian" style with all chinoiserie banished from his classic rooms.

Despite design changes in the 18th century, the love of delicate colors remained constant, as did the fondness for gleaming surfaces and sparkling crystal (Plate 144). Whether in rococo or classic designs, colors were melting pastels, used with slight but authoritative touches of vermilion or dark blue. Fabrics were silky, and like the mirrors and crystal chandeliers, were light reflecting.

When asked to exhibit a flower-show table decoration "in the 18th-century manner," one should concentrate on this quality of "glistering" elegance. To require complete authenticity in regard to table appointments would not be wise unless one were working on a special project, a museum fete, let us say, where actual examples of the period might be available. Even so, there are few museum collections which could produce enough 18th-century silver, porcelain, and crystal to set a complete table, whether of the rococo or classic period.

The more one searches for information about table decoration of past centuries, the more one realizes that a "period" table at the flower show should not be expected to be authentic to the last detail. It would be an arduous task involving exhaustive research for both exhibitor and judge, and a schedule should ask for the *spirit* rather than the *manner* of a period to allow more freedom of interpretation.

What one can do is to steep oneself in the spirit of the chosen style as, once its atmosphere is deeply understood, a pervading sense of its character can often be conveyed without actually using objects of the period at all. One would, of course, try to find table appointments which shared some basic quality of design or color with the originals, but even good reproductions lack the perfection of the real thing. It would be better to emphasize some characteristic of the period which might be more easily duplicated. In addition to the use of delicate colors and light-reflecting surfaces, one might give a clever impression of the spirit of the 18th century by choosing flowers that have the smooth, glossy texture of porcelain and arranging them in close formation with little or no foliage, as in an 18th-century vase of porcelain flowers. This bit of *trompe l'oeil,* in reverse, would be truly in the spirit of the period when to fool the eye was a passion (Plate 145) and porcelain flowers were the height of luxury. Some waxy, pure white cactus dahlias were once so arranged in an antique Chinese porcelain bowl. At a distance it seemed that the flowers could not be real, but on examination one discovered that they were; whereupon the reaction was one of surprise and pleasure at their exquisite freshness and perfection. Surely this would be as much of an "agreeable deception" today, and as unexpected as it was to be fooled by silk or porcelain flowers in the 18th century.

PLATE 130: Dutch "Still Life," by Floris van Schooten. Note the typical 17th-century display of raw and preserved fruits in beautiful delft containers. Of interest also are the dark, patterned tablecloth, and the lovely porcelain dish mounted on a silver-gilt stand. *(From* La Nature Morte de l'Antiquité a Nos Jours, *by Charles Sterling, Paris, 1952; present owner of painting unknown)*

PLATE 131: "Gothic" wreath. This wreath is not really Gothic and is not even really a wreath since flowers and leaves are both in water. But the innocent freshness and wide-eyed charm of the semi-double silver moon roses against the broad rough leaves of applemint have a quality of design found in Gothic sculpture. Today with our training of hand and eye from the flower show, we are quick to see design analogies and to convert them into a contemporary idiom. (*Arrangement by the author; photograph by Francis Lambert*)

PLATE 132: A conversation piece. Of the 17th century, this is hardly to be duplicated outside a museum today. An ostrich egg imaginatively mounted in silver gilt makes an amusing ewer. English, 1680. *(Museum of Fine Arts, Boston)*

PLATE 133: "Still Life," by Pieter Claesz; Dutch, *c.* 1630. This painting not only shows characteristic 17th-century pewter and glassware but a handsome lace-edged tablecloth laid over a velvet or silk cloth of a dark color. The lace is dyed to match the undercloth, in a slightly lighter shade of brownish red. The round individual loaf of bread is typical of those seen in many illustrations of tables from the Middle Ages through the 17th century. Sweetmeats in fancy shapes are on the plate at left. Coloring is a typically somber 17th-century combination of dull reds, red-browns, and lemon yellow with the dark gray of the pewter and the pale greenish white of the glassware. The goblets have heavy knobs on the stems to assure a firm grasp by a slightly fuddled drinker. Note the ornamentation of the handles of the spoon and knife. *(Art Institute of Chicago)*

PLATE 134: The Boxford Room, now at the Museum of Fine Arts, Boston. Here is a display of 17th-century American silver on a table covered with an Oriental rug. This was a very fashionable way to cover a table between meals. At meal time a white linen cloth was usually used on top, letting the rug show below. The owner of this 17th-century house in Boxford, near Boston, would have been very proud of his fine sugar box, his salver and great tankard, as well as the smaller accessories. Notice the candlesticks and the handsome delft bowl on the side table. *(Museum of Fine Arts, Boston)*

PLATE 135: A "banketting" dish from a set depicting the twelve months; owned by Governor Winslow, 1595–1655. The decoration is an engraving pasted on the rim of the dish and includes a verse to be read or sung after dessert. *(Pilgrim Hall, Plymouth, Massachusetts)*

PLATE 136: "A British Family at Tea" in the early 18th century. They proudly display the new type of silver made for the service of the fashionable new beverage, still an expensive luxury though not as prohibitive as it had been in the 17th century. Silver shapes are simple and based on the shapes of Chinese porcelain used for this purpose. In the paintings each member of the family tries to find the best way of holding the delicate little cups of Oriental porcelain. *(Victoria & Albert Museum, London, Crown Copyright)*

PLATE 137: Group of 18th-century English porcelain. Graceful shapes, rococo curves, and a gleaming surface are characteristic. *(Museum of Fine Arts, Boston)*

PLATE 138: "Girl in a Swing," Chelsea porcelain, *c.* 1751. All-white porcelain was favored at this date because of its capacity to reflect light. *(Museum of Fine Arts, Boston)*

PLATE 139: Detail of an asymmetrical rococo surtout by Weye. This is á section of the German silver-
gilt surtout-de-table, 1757–59, shown in Plate 68.
(Courtesy, Wadsworth Athenaeum, Hartford)

PLATE 140: Pair of two light Irish glass
candelabra, 18th century. A new method
of heavy cutting developed during the
second half of the century brought out
the full brilliance of the glass, greatly
increasing the illumination obtained by
wax candles. This pair has deep blue
canopies and pale amber drops. *(Corning
Museum of Glass, New York)*

PLATE 141: French party in the Chinese manner, an 18th-century wash drawing by Le Prince. *(Collection of Mrs. A. Everett Austin, Jr.)*

PLATE 142: Classic tureen for the table, design by Robert Adam, 1773. *(Courtesy, Trustees of Sir John Soane's Museum, London)*

PLATE 143: Adam dining room from Lansdowne House, London, 1765–68 (now at the Metropolitan Museum of Art, New York). The designer was right in feeling that in a room like this, furniture and table appointments should be in the classic taste. But until Adam himself designed them, rococo silver and chinoiserie designs on furniture continued to be used and ladies still wore the full-skirted gowns of the rococo period. In the last quarter of the century, however, fashion and the decorative arts caught up and his classic rooms were graced by ladies in straight, high-waisted dresses inspired by the antique, while classic designs in furniture, silver, and other appointments were preferred. *(Photograph from a recent exhibit by the Costume Institute at the Metropolitan Museum of Art, New York)*

PLATE 144: A Wedgwood creamware dessert service from the Gorely collection. Instead of silver, this 18th-century setting uses table appointments made of creamware such as candlesticks, coasters, nut dishes, and even the handles of knives and forks. It was an innovation so much admired when introduced that silver almost went out of fashion. *(Courtesy of Mr. and Mrs. Charles P. Gorely, Jr.; arrangement by the author; photograph by Zitso Studio)*

PLATE 145: Trompe l'oeil, or fool the eye; Niderviller, French, 18th-century pottery. This type of deception was popular through the 17th, 18th, and early 19th centuries. This covered cup and plate are painted to look like wood with objects painted on so realistically that one might try to pick them up. *(Museum of Fine Arts, Boston)*

PLATE 146: Silver resist luster tea set, *c.* 1840. Note the classic influence in the oval shape of the tea pot and in the palmettes dividing the flowered panels. *(Bennington Museum, Bennington, Vermont; gift of Mrs. Jesse N. Mallory, Sr.)*

PLATE 147: Chinese Export porcelain of Fitzhugh design with pagoda center; *c.* 1810. *(Museum of Fine Arts, Boston)*

PLATE 148: Gothic detail in an English stoneware pitcher of 1842. Figures are too small for the niches, and crockets too big, looking uncomfortable as they are forced to bend backward to conform to the shape of the vessel. The whole conception, though pedantic in feeling, is inaccurate and shows a lack of understanding of the spirit of Gothic design. *(Metropolitan Museum of Art, New York; gift of E. H. Hayle, 1927)*

PLATE 149: Pair of French cartonage dessert stands, *c.* 1810. This pair shows the amount of detail and perfection lavished upon these replicas of more expensive stands. *(Courtesy, Louis Lyons, New York City)*

PLATE 150: Plate from the Flora Danica service. Notice the meticulously painted design of mushrooms. *(Danish Museum of Decorative Art, Copenhagen)*

PLATE 151: English porcelain plate, signed T. Baxter, 1808. Baxter, whose signature it bears, was famous for his realistic rendering of shells satisfying the most ardent conchologist. *(Victoria & Albert Museum, London, Crown Copyright)*

PLATE 152: "Extravagant prettiness." This Victorian rococo of a silver epergne was made in 1840 by a nephew of Paul Storr. (*Museum of Fine Arts, Boston*)

PLATE 153: A grandiose surtout-de-table; made by Christofle, French silversmiths, for Napoleon III in 1853. (See fruit stand from this same surtout, Plate 64.) This was exhibited in a Second Empire setting at the Musée des Arts Décoratifs in Paris in 1964. Plates are reproductions of china of the period. They rest on antique silver plates from a private collection. *(Courtesy, Christofle, Paris)*

PLATE 154: A late 19th-century French table. Note the epergne of fruit and flowers in "La Desserte" by Matisse. *(From the collection of Mr. and Mrs. Stavros Niarchos, Paris; photograph, courtesy of M. Knoedler and Company, Inc.)*

PLATE 155: Lily pad bowl of New York State glass, *c.* 1840. *(Bennington Museum, Bennington, Vermont; collection of Mr. and Mrs. Joseph W. Limric)*

The 19th Century

It is axiomatic that every generation repudiates the most treasured household possessions of a generation or two before. Sentimental grandmothers and great-grandmothers who insisted upon saving everything with family associations, even if their daughters relegated them to the attic, may today be thanked for holding on to that pink luster tea set, the "Chelsea sprig" china, or Chinese Export porcelain which their descendants now enjoy, while their friends collect such things avidly at ever increasing prices (Plates 146 and 147).

These same descendants may still scorn the Haviland and Limoges china, Tiffany glass, and Art Nouveau table appointments of the late 19th century. Now, however, Art Nouveau relics have begun to emerge from the attic, not to go, as formerly, to the rummage sale, for they now command high prices and are being put to new uses by the avant-garde in ways that would surprise their original owners.

Apparently it takes about a hundred years before a fashion which has been rejected and all but forgotten can be looked at with a fresh eye and re-evaluated, and then it is often appreciated for quite different reasons from those that made it seem desirable in its own day. *Cartonage,* which was, in the early 19th century simply a means of providing a fashionable centerpiece at modest expense, is now a collector's item, valued for its rarity, its delicately classic detail, and for the exquisite perfection of its workmanship so astonishing when one considers that it was only intended to be an inexpensive substitute for porcelain or gilt bronze (Plate 149). Parian "images" for the table were, when they first appeared in the 1840's, desired chiefly because they looked like marble and imitated Greek sculpture, since the neo-Greek style was then in full force. Parian, with its slight "smear" of glaze over the plain white porcelain, gave the softly lustrous texture of polished marble. In fact, it was admired because it did not have the high glaze of porcelain, now *demodé* because it was considered to reflect too much light, or the dullness of biscuit porcelain which reflected no light at all. Parian figures today are valued not for any of these reasons but because they have a distinction all their own and are appropriate in a neoclassic setting.

The increasing necessity in the 19th century to imitate more expensive materials was an indication of the basic insecurity of the newly affluent middle classes. Unlike the 18th-century "curioso," who was so-called because he was intellectually curious and culturally aware, always seeking the unusual and the unique, the newly rich of the 19th century were a little afraid of being "different." What they wanted was to be "correct," to play safe with known and proven fashions.

In the first quarter of the century the safe and accepted thing was the "classic taste" which was well established and admired fairly consistently with little change except for the addition of Egyptian motifs, an influence largely due to the Nile campaigns of Napoleon, and in England, to Nelson's great Egyptian victory. There was, to be sure, a rash of chinoiserie and other Orientalia, thanks to the Prince Regent's fondness for exotic design at the Royal Pavilion, built for him by John Nash in "Indian" style, and also a definite increase in the neo-Gothic movement which had begun in the 18th century. This last romantic mood went along with the literature of the day which dwelt upon medieval chivalry, crumbling castles, and ruined abbeys "well overgrown with ivy and properly inhabited by Choughs and Daws," with perhaps a hermit in a cave to give the appropriately "horrid" fascination.

It is curious that all these influences eventually invaded the field of table decoration, but they did. Egyptian sphinxes supported candelabra and silver centerpieces, while scarabs and lotus motifs vied with Greek key and honeysuckle patterns to ornament classic shapes in both silver and porcelain. As for the Gothic trend, teapots, bowls, and pitchers often had cusped and crocketed panels with Gothic figures and tracery (Plate 148), while porcelain plates, flower vases, cups, and bowls were painted with landscape views of ivy-draped castles and ancient ruins. Even an "image" of the hermit in his cave may have been recommended for the garden-parterre centerpiece since he was an admired feature of the fashionable 19th-century naturalistic garden.

The French Empire style, with its heavily scaled Egyptiana, was a more grandiose interpretation of the classic than the delicate Adam style of the 18th century. Empire was much admired everywhere in Europe and also in America where French fashions were much in favor.

Another important influence was an increasing interest in natural history. This really began in the 17th century, was taken up by the aristocratic curioso in the 18th, and became widely popular in the early 19th century. Scientific study, not only of plants but also of birds, rocks, and shells became more and more the fashion, and this trend was soon seized upon by makers of pottery and porcelain, perhaps accelerated because of the renown of the remarkable Flora Danica dessert service made in Copenhagen at the end of the 18th century. The designs for this famous service of over a thousand pieces (originally intended as a gift from the Danish government to Catherine II of Russia but not finished until 1802, six years after her death) were taken from a great 18th-century work on the Danish flora, a subject doubtless selected because the director of the Copenhagen factory was himself interested in botany (Plate 150). English and Continental factories were quick to appreciate the appeal of realistically painted shells (Plate 151; see also Plate 96) as well as plants, birds, and even insects in the style of the illustrations in contemporary books on these subjects, while Wedgwood used authentic shell shapes for creamware dessert dishes which delighted customers able to identify them by their Latin names.

A series of revivals of historic styles began in the 1830's, perhaps because they were considered comfortably familiar and of suitably impressive status value. Italian Renaissance, Elizabethan, Francis I, Louis XIV, and neo-Greek each took its turn in favor and was unmistakably stamped with the rather self-conscious, slightly inaccurate, but earnestly pedantic mark of the Victorian designer. There was also a resurgence of the ever-admired rococo which was no doubt welcome for its gaiety and freedom. The Victorians gave it what one writer on 19th-century antiques has described as "an extravagant prettiness" (Plate 152), rather different from the verve of the original style but pleasant after an overwhelming dose of grandeur and a classicism which had become rather pompous. The elaborate silver centerpiece made for Napoleon III in 1853 by Christofle of Paris, for example, was replete with symbolic figures, agricultural attributes, and other pseudo-classic ornamentation. Plate 153 shows this centerpiece as it was exhibited at the Musée des Arts Décoratifs in 1964, appropriately festooned with the cabbage roses so popular in its day and displayed in a typical Second Empire setting against a background of the inevitable potted palms. There was fine craftsmanship in this grandiose piece but the attempt to "get everything in" (which was apt to be a failing of designers in the last half of the 19th century) defeated its effectiveness (Plate 64).

To evaluate the many and varied products of the late 19th century requires keen selective judgment. Some tablewares were made in obvious appeal to the untutored taste of the parvenu, who sometimes mistook the gaudy for the grand. Colors were often unpleasantly muddy. Rita Wellman, in *Victoria Royal,* says of the typical Victorian interior that "there are numerous colors here and there but they are swallowed up by each other, so that the general effect is like that of a palette on which all the contents of the paint tubes have been scrambled together . . . producing something that has no color at all." Designers of tablewares, with a confusion shared by their customers, not only muddled their colors but frequently mixed historic styles to the point of absurdity. At other times individual artists interpreted the prevailing mode with competence and style, maintaining a high level of craftsmanship as well.

It was when the machine entered the picture that the real trouble began, for the machine could not match the spontaneity of work done by hand. Take the popular lily-pad pattern which appeared in mid-19th-century American glass. Its design was outstandingly spirited and lively at a time when so many crafts were being invaded by the machine. Its success was probably due to the crafts-man's sheer pleasure in swirling and manipulating a separate "gather" of glass by way of surface ornamentation for this was, as one modern glass technician suggests, "a fun thing, easy to do with glass" and it was perhaps accidental that the result resembled a lily pad (Plate 155). The combination of a fresh idea and the technique best fitted to carry it out is hard to beat and a good craftsman's control of his material gives it a certain joyous quality quite lacking in machine work in endless imitation of historic designs.

Table settings at the end of the century were either incredibly fussy or earn-estly "artistic." Pseudo-period silver, hand-painted china, and art glass might be displayed on a tablecloth crossed by wide satin ribbons with a bow on each corner "like a little girl's sash." Or they might be used by followers of the Arts and Crafts Movement (instigated by William Morris and others in protest against the relentless encroachment of the machine age) on a table runner of pongee, hand stenciled with conventionalized tulips or wild roses. The table runner was then, in the 1880's and '90's, a daring innovation. Not so long before, in 1861, an authority on household management had stated firmly that "beautiful white damask and a green cloth [of felt!] underneath" were "indispensable." To be allowed to show the bare table before the service of the dessert was the beginning of the emancipation of the hostess from ponderous and unnecessary coverings not only for the table but also for the room in general, and for her-self.

The stuffy, cluttered Victorian interior—with its confusion of patterns, its dark, dreary colors, and its heavy draperies over lace curtains, window shades or blinds would stifle us today since, thanks to modern design and a knowledge of modern hygiene, we have grown accustomed to fresh air, clear colors, sun-lit rooms, simpler forms, and open spaces without ornament. But one aspect of the period which is longed for by many, perhaps because it is so seldom realized, is the *fin-de-siècle* atmosphere of quiet decorum and leisurely elegance, an aura of graciousness lightly sugar coated with remembrance of things past (Plate 154).

Gone, alas, is the readily available service which made that atmosphere possible at the turn of the century, but an illusion of it can still be evoked, when desired, by a bit of clever stage-management. I know one Southern hostess who achieves this with the simplest means. Heavy taffeta curtains of *bois-de-rose* with wide-pleated ruffles hang in deep folds in the double doorway between her living room and the dining room. When dinner is announced by the one servant, the guests notice for the first time that the curtains have been dramatically looped back with gilt tie-backs, revealing the Victorian mahogany table resplendent with its silver and crystal of ante-bellum days. In the center of the table a silver epergne holds pink camellias and bunches of violets, and though the meal itself may be relatively simple, the romantic setting of Southern hospitality puts the guests in a gracious mood, making the dinner memorable.

Art Nouveau

The only truly original style to emerge in the 19th century was the romantic, naturalistic trend known as Art Nouveau which evolved at the end of the century and enjoyed a few decades of exuberant expression. It was rightly called "a new art" because, being creative rather than imitative, the approach was new to 19th-century artists and designers. Elements from the past, rather than being copied without thought or understanding, were now adapted and modified for a creative purpose. For example, the sweeping lines of the baroque and the more playful, curvilinear forms of the rococo were simplified and expressed in a new way with a fresh appreciation of their feeling of movement and sense of freedom.

Perhaps the greatest source of inspiration for this new approach was the impact of Japanese art, exhibited for the first time in the West at the International Exhibition in London in 1862, although occasional Japanese importations had been seen and studied with interest by a number of artists in Paris, including Whistler, very shortly before that date. Japanese lacquers, wood carvings, and prints, with their asymmetrical organization of forms full of dynamic tensions, crisp fluid lines, and broad two-dimensional patterns opened the eyes of Western artists to the decorative potentialities of plant life rendered realistically as surface ornamentation.

Designers of glass, metal ware, ceramics, textiles, wallpaper, and furniture found that the spirit of this new style filled their needs for a new approach to the decorative arts. Table appointments soon reflected the trend, using the controlled "whiplash" line, as it has been called, in the ornamentation of china, silver, and glass. Plant forms were not confined to stylized areas, as in the Flora Danica service, but slender stems swayed up from a single point of growth to flow over a dish or pitcher as would a living plant. Often the shape of the vessel itself assumed an organic form like a lily or tulip or the calyx of a flower. There was a vitality in this new expression of a living line not to be seen again until the appearance of the "free forms" of modern design.

Moreover, the simplicity, drama, and clarity of Japanese prints with their elimination of unnecessary detail and the glimpses they afforded of uncluttered Japanese interiors had a tremendous effect upon architecture and decoration, leading to the eventual banishment of the antimacassar, the whatnot, and other aspects of Victorian fussiness. Probably one of the most important contributions of Art Nouveau to its own time and to the future was its achievement of a unified harmony of colors and forms in interior design which had been woefully lacking through the last half of the 19th century.

Today, if we collect Art Nouveau, it is either because we appreciate its significance as a vital, historic style and enjoy tracking down its best examples which have real charm, freedom of expression, and fine craftsmanship, or because we find it amusing to use an occasional bizarre selection as a conversation piece (Plate 156). In either case, we would not necessarily recreate its original background unless there were some reason for authenticity as, for example, in the decor so superbly provided by Cecil Beaton for the movie version of *My Fair Lady*. We might prefer to devise a new setting to point up the element of surprise which is so much a part of Art Nouveau's current appeal. Needless to say, we should avoid the fringe aspects of lower middle-class objects which the industrial age turned out in frantic imitation to meet popular demand when the style was at its height and of which, unfortunately, many horrible examples still abound (Plate 157).

Art glass, though sometimes in this category, is, at its best, rather touching in its wistful search for the color and natural beauty so much needed at the dawn of the mechanical era. One can imagine selecting individual examples of Peachblow, Amberina, the René Lalique pieces, or Tiffany's iridescent peacock-feathered glass with their attenuated, flower-like, or bulbous shapes, to display on shelves against a background of soft green, dusty pink, or turquoise blue. Or perhaps one could place four or five "trumpet" or "lily" vases of assorted heights in an asymmetrical group down the center of the table like a grove of wine-glass elms (Plate 158), each vase holding a fountain of nicotiana, fuchsias, or spray carnations high above the eye level of seated guests.

A new and better use than their original function for the really charming little triangular, frilled, or square-topped toothpick holders of art glass would be to fill them with small flowers like grape hyacinths or lilies of the valley, placing them in a circle around a tall fruit compote. Approached with imagination, there are many uses for the long-neglected style of Art Nouveau.

Colors favored at the height of the fashion, though to us a little timid and tinged with sentimentality, must surely have seemed fresh and charming to the Victorians so long accustomed to a stodgy diet of gloomy chocolate hues, dark reds, and frog-pond greens. Art Nouveau brought flat, pastel colors: silver gray, pale greens and blues, muted reds, dim orange, pink, mauve, violet, and creamy white. More sophisticated was the use of white against white, a combination beloved by Whistler and used in his white dining room and in several of his paintings which may have inspired Art Nouveau designers. A dining room by the Belgian designer and architect Henri Van de Velde at the turn of the century (Plate 159) has a subtle white on white scheme. The slightly deeper tone of the upholstery of the white butterfly-shaped chairs points up their delicately curving wings, and other white furniture against the white walls echoes the graceful linear detail.

Not all Art Nouveau color was pale, however. Bakst, scenic and costume designer for the Russian ballet just after the turn of the century, used strong, clear colors with bold Slavic impact. Poiret, too, preferred a more daring use of color. *Memorable Balls* by James Laver gives a vivid description of the famous Poiret Ball which had the exotic splendor of a fete at the court of Harun-al-Rashid and which was the talk of Paris in 1910. Poiret loved to handle color with *brio* but he insisted that he was not influenced by the Russian ballet, merely bored with the monotonous pale tints so much in fashion. As he expressed it, "*nuances de cuisse de nymphe* [delicately translated in England as maiden's blush], lilacs, swooning mauves, tender blue hortensias [hydrangeas], niles, maizes, straws, all that was soft, washed out, insipid was held in honor. I threw into this sheepcote," he says wickedly, "a few rough wolves: reds, greens, violets, royal blues that made all the rest sing aloud . . . the morbid mauves were hunted out of existence." Here is a color scheme not only lovely for a ball but well worth trying for a flower arrangement in an Art Nouveau setting, or in an "arranger's" garden!

The 20th Century

Table centerpieces in the first decade of the 20th century were apt to be routine and unimaginative. In winter a silver "fern dish" was an easy solution for every day, perhaps to be replaced by a silver bowl of carnations or roses on "company" occasions. In summer a glass bowl would hold garden roses, stuffed into a foundation of gypsophila; or a solid mound of nasturtiums, sweet peas, or other annuals might be admired. In the autumn the bowl held fruit, not "arranged" but simply there to be eaten if anyone felt so inclined.

In certain rarified circles an occasional avant-garde hostess might attempt a "Japanese" arrangement, inspired by Josiah Conder's book on *The Flowers of Japan and the Art of Floral Arrangement* (1891) but if this were done, it was more often because it was the fashion of the moment than because of any real appreciation of the beauty of line or any understanding of the technique or symbolism involved. In 1900, in *Home and Garden,* Gertrude Jekyll, English artist and horticulturist, remarked on this fad and expressed herself as doubtful if it had value for anyone not blessed with a sense of "good drawing" or a knowledge of Japanese tradition. On the other hand she deplored the sort of overloaded flower arrangement constructed on the premise that "you cannot have too much of a good thing," which she thought a "mischievous" teaching. Such bouquets, she felt, often made a room appear "less a room than a thicket." She wisely counseled that, "As in all matters of decoration . . . one of the first and wholesomest laws is that of restraint and moderation."

However, the great vogue of this decade was for Art Nouveau which was exuberant rather than restrained. To be in the height of fashion one would set one's table with china, art glass, and silver, either in naturalistic shapes or ornamented with the organic flow of line typical of this exotic style. Flowers and/or peacock feathers might be artlessly arranged in trumpet vases, or fruit might be displayed in a compote or epergne of Lalique or Tiffany glass. Not only did this fashion sweep all Europe and America but it is interesting that even the Orient, whose own art contributed so much to Art Nouveau, was itself occasionally influenced in return by Western ideas and interpretations (Plate 160). This, however, was probably more in the interest of trade than because of any admiration of the Western fashion. For their own use, Orientals usually—quite rightly—prefer their own traditions.

By 1912 many voices other than Gertrude Jekyll's were pleading for moderation. Art Nouveau had played itself out and an austere simplicity was suddenly

PLATE 156: Venetian glass version of Art Nouveau. The swirling lines of a windblown flower are romantic with a touch of baroque drama. This late 19th-century compote of translucent yellow and clear glass is splashed with green and silver. *(Corning Museum of Glass, New York)*

PLATE 157: Florid example of industrial design. Here is a tasteless combination of historic forms with an attempt to imitate the naturalistic detail of Art Nouveau. Craftsmanship, also, is at a low ebb, most obvious in the rubbery modeling of the insipid cupids. *(From a late 19th-century catalogue of silverware)*

PLATE 158: Four lily or trumpet vases of Amberina glass. This was a popular form in the early 20th century, in silver as well as glass. *(From* The Identification of American Art Glass *by Richard Carter Barret, Bennington Museum)*

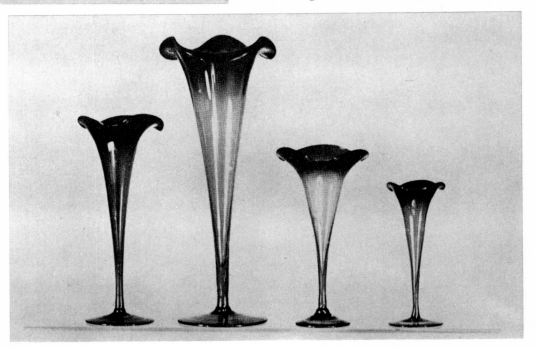

PLATE 159: White on white dining room. The subtle revelation of white forms, almost a cult with avant-garde artists today, was appreciated in this 1910 room design in Art Nouveau style. *(Courtesy, Verlag Gerd Hatje, publishers of* Art Nouveau *by Robert Schmutzler, 1964)*

PLATE 160: Chinese bronze bowl of irregular contour. This is an example of European Art Nouveau influence in the Orient. The detachable lid of silver is an openwork pattern of swirling lines suggesting water ripples around sculptured silver water lilies, lily pads, and a turtle. *(Collection of Mrs. Edward F. Bowman; photograph by George M. Cushing)*

PLATE 161: Lenox porcelain service plate. This piece is from a set purchased for the White House in the Wilson Administration, 1913–21. *(White House Historical Association)*

PLATE 162: A glass plate, "The Broken Bridge," from the Orrefors factory, designed by Edward Hald in 1923. The piece was considered "futuristic," a term connoting a departure from traditional forms and an expression of the dynamic energy and movement of mechanical processes. Although today we get the message of a chaotic occurrence, we see it chiefly as an amusingly imaginative, decorative pattern in the modern spirit. Japanese asymmetry may have played a part in its inspiration. (*Nationalmuseum, Stockholm*)

PLATE 163: Two examples of Swedish topaz glass. Here is the commonest glass made interesting in shape and color. (*From* The Modern Decorative Arts of Sweden *by Erik Wettergren, Malmo Museum, 1926*)

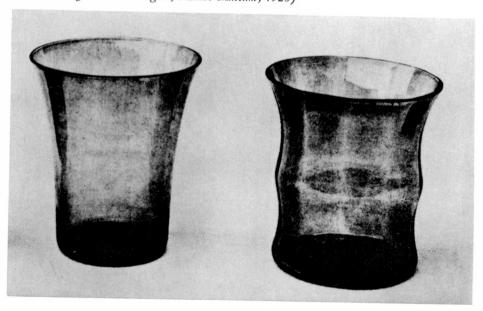

PLATE 164: Swedish silver coffee service by Jacob Angman, 1925. Observe the clean, uncluttered lines of modern design. *(Malmo Museum, Sweden)*

PLATE 165: French surrealist table. The fantastic and incongruous imagery of a surrealist painting is suggested in this amusing table staged at a 1950 exhibit at the Musée des Arts Décoratifs in Paris, by French industrial designers. *(From Art et Industrie, March, 1951)*

PLATE 166: A white-on-white centerpiece, suggested by an exhibit of modern art. *(Arrangement by the author; photograph by George M. Cushing)*

PLATE 167: Anatolian copper; four-wheeled cart and warriors, *c.* 2100 B.C. Here are ancient objects which look modern and would surely be a conversation piece on a modern table. *(Museum of Fine Arts, Boston)*

PLATE 168: Modern cook-and-serve casserole with high style. *(Courtesy, Mrs. Hardwick Moseley)*

PLATE 169: Modern sculpture centerpiece. On an artist's table an amusing and imaginative piece of modern sculpture of scrap metal makes a conversation-provoking centerpiece whether with modern pottery or, as here, antique Chinese Export ware. *(Collection of Mrs. Edward F. Bowman, sculpture by Richard A. Fishman; photograph by George M. Cushing)*

demanded. In America this was at first expressed, not in the stark "essentials" of modern design, a movement still remote from popular acceptance, but in a dawning appreciation of our own national heritage. Forward-looking people who had perhaps found Art Nouveau too restless to live with comfortably, saw the need for change and began to haunt country auctions where, for a song, they were able to pick up simple early American furniture of pine or maple, colonial silver, pewter, "treen," earthenware, and other 17th- and 18th-century artifacts. Antique collecting soon became an avid pursuit, prices advancing, naturally, to meet the demand. Young homemakers raided family attics for forgotten treasures, pouncing with particular relish upon anything they thought "quaint," even if on occasion, crude.

Derelict colonial houses also began to be rescued and carefully restored, their pine-sheathed kitchens transformed into charming dining rooms with a great fireplace making a perfect setting for a collection of wrought-iron implements and pewter tankards. Used with pride on the table or displayed in a corner cupboard, there might be, along with pewter and wooden ware, some of the grander possessions which well-to-do colonists imported from England or Holland: Dutch or English delft; porcelain from the East Indies; plain stoneware (salt-glaze) and English Staffordshire, also imported before the Revolution. It was indeed fortunate that this newly awakened appreciation of a more tranquil and controlled form of design reminded us of this heritage and that countless 17th- and 18th-century treasures were thus saved from neglect and outright destruction before we were caught up in some of the more stimulating and exotic influences of modern art.

In our flower shows of the 1920's, when the arrangement classes were first added to the traditional horticultural exhibits, the trend for simplicity was soon reflected, and table decorations shown often used the more unpretentious wares, sometimes converted to uses that would have astonished the colonists . . . perhaps an earthenware pudding mold or mortar to hold flowers or a bowl made from a great burl of curly maple, intended for the kitchen, used in the center of the table to hold fruit. Flower designs found in old prints and chintz patterns furnished inspiration for table arrangements at the flower show in an attempt to foster an appreciation of casual charm expressed in a clear and ordered pattern. There was no thought of exhibiting "period" tables at this time. Simplicity was admired not because it was old fashioned but because it was the "new look." Restraint was in the air, and the Garden Club of America, leader of the rapidly growing garden-club movement, was encouraging not only discipline in garden design but a more studied approach to flower arrangement as well.

Meanwhile shops offered plenty of formal table appointments appealing to those not interested in the quest of the quaint or the "craze for the crude," but even the most elegant and expensive of these followed the demand for clean, uncluttered lines. By 1912 the "new" plain flat silver, based on colonial examples, was replacing heavy, *repoussé,* Victorian styles or the meandering patterns of Art Nouveau, and fine tableware like Lenox porcelain was sometimes entirely unadorned to dramatize its "egg shell" color and texture. If ornamented at all, there was usually a narrow gold rim at the edge with perhaps a wider band of color inside. President Woodrow Wilson, during his administration (1913–21) ordered for the White House a handsome Lenox dinner service with the seal of the United States in the center and a broad border of dark blue within the outer gold rim. This was the first American-made china to be ordered for White House use (Plate 161).

Though a quiet, rather unsophisticated simplicity was the prevailing trend in the 1920's, we were due for a violent upheaval in the next decade, for the yeasty ferment which had been brewing in the world of art since the turn of the century at last burst upon our consciousness. Exhibitions of modern paintings, sculpture, and industrial design, art books, and popular home magazines (the latter increasingly competitive and influential in the wide dissemination of the newest ideas in decoration gleaned from world sources) brought greater familiarity with modern art and more understanding of the turbulent new "isms' and changing experiments in methods and attitudes toward all the arts. The initial strangeness of impressionism, cubism, expressionism, abstraction, and other movements gradually seemed less bewildering and even became fascinating. Designers were naturally the first to be intrigued, and they seized upon the decorative aspects of modern painting, and experimented with the imaginative uses of design and color found there. Artists and architects began to design for the industrial arts, learning to work with, instead of against, the machine. The words "streamlined," "functional," and "free form" were added to the decorator's vocabulary. There was a growing sense of exciting creative activity which soon communicated itself to the general public.

Perhaps most influential was the great international exhibition of decorative arts held in Paris in 1925. Here, although signed pieces of art glass by the famous French designers Gallé, Marinot, and other artists were much admired, the greatest excitement was in the new approach to industrial art as exhibited by factories where fine artists were employed not only to make a few expensive, hand-crafted objects for a limited market but also to produce simple, inexpensive artifacts for everyday use.

For example, Simon Gate and Edward Hald, two gifted and imaginative artists at the Orrefors factory in Sweden, exhibited not only their superb engraved glass (Plate 162) and a stunning version of deep-cut crystal (Plate 107), similar to Renaissance intaglio in technique yet modern in inspiration. In addition, these same artists also gave subtle new forms and beauty of color to the cheapest material, soda-glass, from which the common people were accustomed to drink their beer (Plate 163). Hitherto completely undistinguished, these everyday glasses now appeared in attractive shapes and in deep sea green, golden brown, or smoke color, bringing household objects of beauty within the reach of all. Swedish ceramic factories, too, employed their best artists to design for mass production as well as for their more expensive wares, and the owner of one factory found this venture so profitable that he was often heard to refer to his line of cheap and pretty pottery as his Ford. Czechoslovakian manufacturers, in a joyous burst of enthusiasm under their new Republic of 1918, exerted skill and imagination in the production of low-priced pottery, glass, and other everyday tablewares. The direct, refreshing character of their work, reflecting their peasant heritage of bold Slavic color and inventive design, appealed greatly to modern taste. Mexico, also, offered crude but attractive table glass, traditional native pottery, and an elegant greenish black pottery of great distinction.

These handsome, inexpensive foreign wares not only found a ready market in America but also greatly influenced and stimulated American designers. Although American manufacturers were unable to compete with Europe in low cost merchandise, our best artists gave more and more attention to industrial design, as was shown in an exhibition of contemporary work, "The Architect and the Industrial Arts," held at the Metropolitan Museum of Art in New York in 1929. For this exhibition Eliel Saarinen, the well-known architect, designed a dining room for which he created not only the architectural background but also all the furnishings including the table appointments. His designs for the china were carried out by Lenox; his glass, executed by the Steuben division of the Corning Glass Works; and his silver, both flat silver and a handsome centerpiece, was executed by several established American silver firms. All these designs showed the new feeling for the elimination of unnecessary detail and, as Saarinen himself expressed it in the catalogue of the exhibit, were arrived at by searching for "an expression of contemporary life and modern points of view," beginning with simple forms and then "looking for truth and logic in regard both to construction and to material." This philosophy is the basic foundation of modern art as we know it today.

Although 20th-century forms were more and more severe and stark, modern color was exuberant, and the most noticeable manifestation of the influence of modern painting in the 1920's was the insistent introduction of color into every phase of everyday life. The Impressionists' fresh, sun-drenched, three-dimensional colors appeared on walls, in furnishings, and on the table. That sacrosanct and hitherto "indispensable white tablecloth" now ventured forth in peach, pale blue, and Nile green and, later, in rich dark hues which had not been seen on the dining table since the 17th century. In glassware the subtle, smoky tones of Swedish glass were adopted, followed in the 1940's by strong deep colors, bolder and more uninhibited, lifted from the canvases of modern painters by adventurous decorators and designers.

Not all modern color was brilliant or violent, however. The Orphists used "mood colors" in rhythmic sequences, likened to symphonic music by their devotees, and the abstractionists, while often vigorous and emotional with reds, orange, purple, electric blues, and sharp yellows were sometimes tender with pinks, "linen blues, water greens, straw yellows" and white. The cubists, to emphasize their major preoccupation with form, used restrained browns, ochers, sand, and other earth colors with a dramatic use of black and white which influenced industrial design to such an extent that the 1930's have been disparagingly referred to as the "Beige Decade."[3] In reality, however, the cubists' sensitive use of rather somber harmonies was their finest and most enduring contribution to modern art. A color scheme taken from a painting by Braque, Juan Gris, or Picasso in their cubist period may well be chosen today as inspiration for a table setting in the most modern spirit. There is great subtlety and style in these low-keyed tonalities of grays and browns with occasional touches of dull plum, dusty pink, and olive green, colors often found in attractive table linens, pottery, and glass.

At the flower show, that microcosm of current influences, this vogue for quiet harmonies led to an appreciation of weathered driftwood and dried material, often used on the table in an informal setting. Constance Spry, perceptive English writer on gardening and flower arrangement, also felt this influence and taught us to see beauty in "the quiet, the unobtrusive, the mysterious fritillaries," as well as in green or black hellebores, black violas, decorative kale, and echeveria; gray foliage, lichened branches and sepia, parchment, or mushroom tonalities in all sorts of dried or semidry material. Exhibitors developed a seeing eye for such subtleties and were ever watchful for unexpectedly decorative possibilities of familiar flowers, perhaps when dormant, or in seed, or when just beginning to unfold.

In table arrangements at the flower show of the 1930's, one could see the influence of modern design as well as of modern color. There was a new interest in form and in open spatial relationships as well as in the asymmetry which the Japanese contributed. It was no coincidence that Japanese flower arrangement, studied so assiduously in the 1930's by flower-show exhibitors, influenced schemes for erstwhile "center" pieces which now were frequently placed off-center, balanced by a group of candlesticks or by an accessory. The Japanese *moribana* type of arrangement, with an asymmetrical grouping in a shallow rectangular container, was also popular in American adaptations for informal tables.

Japanese flower arrangement, now far more intelligently studied than in 1900 (notably in and near New York under the influence and guidance of Mrs. Yoneo Arai, a gifted artist as well as a skilled technician with deep knowledge of Japanese symbolism and tradition) gave us a new conception of the beauty of line and valuable lessons in control of material which contributed to the development of "the American style" of flower arrangement. Basic principles of design from the Occidental point of view were also explored, prompted by John Taylor Arms whose excellent book (written with his wife, Dorothy Noyes Arms) on *Design in Flower Arrangement* gave a clear and helpful analysis of these principles, together with some of the philosophical aspects of design. His book is still used by students of flower arrangement, many of whom would do well to re-read his last chapter which considers the creative element in art so necessary in addition to technique.

Meanwhile manufacturers of table appointments were attempting, not too successfully, to translate the cubes, tubes, cones, and angles of cubist paintings into new forms for tableware. There was a brief vogue for geometric designs or broken, angular patterns. Goblets or candlesticks were often tubular with square or triangular bases. More successful was the sophisticated and suavely polished wooden ware of Russell Wright and the handsome clear, thick glass in expressive forms made by Steuben, which was similar to the earlier glass by the French artist, Marinot. Distinguished designs in the modern spirit were also made in silver, notably in Scandinavia (Plate 164).

In the 1940's there was much interest in exotic objects: Negro, Pre-Columbian, and Oriental forms. Museums sold attractive and inexpensive reproductions of these, and one was not surprised to see them adapted to flower-show use and thence to our tables, either as containers or as accessories. This fascination with the exotic gave rise to the love of the exotic in plant material, now available from the four corners of the earth via airplane. Expanding world trade with its rapid dissemination of ideas, arts, and customs of little-known faraway places added fresh inspiration in form and color. The popular stage and screen productions of *The King and I,* for example, introduced excitingly different color combinations of hot pink and orange or the fantastic multicolored harmonies from the many-layered roofs of Thailand's palaces and temples. Modern chemistry provided synthetic materials for tableware, place mats, and tablecloths many of them well designed and a boon to the busy housewife.

Flower-show schedule-makers vied with one another to invent stimulating classes in table settings for specified occasions—a buffet, a hunt breakfast, a children's party, a stag dinner, a holiday celebration. When rivalry among exhibitors led to a more and more extravagant choice of table appointments, "Economy Tables" were called for to prove that taste and imagination were possible on a limited budget. On the whole these flower-show classes were of great value in the education of public taste, particularly in the '30's and '40's. Since then the overwhelming popularity of these classes has made them inevitably more imitative and rule-bound and the mysteries of "the judging" have unfortunately somewhat alienated the casual spectator. The flower show's sphere of influence on the average person has since been largely taken over, for better or worse, by the popular magazines which, with their lavish "spreads" of color photography, keep the reader supplied with new ideas and alerted to emerging trends. Arrangement classes in the flower show today appeal chiefly to a relatively small but dedicated coterie of exhibitors, many of whom find competitive exhibiting a rewarding hobby and a genuine source of creative satisfaction.

Although in Europe the idea of competitive arrangements at a flower show did not arouse any enthusiasm until the late 1950's, a series of interesting exhibits of table settings were instigated early in that decade by the Musée des Arts Décoratifs in Paris to dramatize and publicize new offerings by the makers of French table appointments. Sometimes these tables had elaborate settings imaginatively recalling specific historic periods. Others were provocatively modern even surrealistic in character. An amusing example combines traditional and futuristic porcelain with heavy crystal on a dark brocade cloth above which, as incongruously as Dali's limp watches on the beach, white plaster arms hold a spirited garland of red peppers lightly caught up by the fingers of the long slender hands (Plate 165). At one of these exhibits, tables were staged against a photomural made from the illustrations in an 18th-century cookbook showing fantastically molded desserts and high pyramids of sweetmeats. On some tables feathers combined with flowers, and a "bouquet" of a cauliflower, artichokes, a pineapple, and sprays of maidenhair fern unexpectedly, yet wittily, embellished a modern rococo tureen with a whimsical exaggeration of rococo curves.

In America we were more literal, both in our period arrangements, which attempted to be authentic, and in our modern arrangements, which adopted a routine stylization seldom really catching the individualistic spirit of modern art.

Interest in period flower arrangement, here, beginning in the late 1940's, led to the appearance of two scholarly books on the history of flower arrangement: *Period Flower Arrangement* by Margaret Fairbanks Marcus (1952) and *A History of Flower Arrangement* by Julia S. Berrall (1953). Both these books contributed much to an understanding of the many imaginative uses of flowers in the past and provided a solid basis for further study. However at that time little definitive information on the history of table decoration was available. There have been, of course, a number of books on contemporary table decoration.

By 1960 there was so great a diversity of influences both in color and in design that it could only result in a need for a more personal and selective study nourished by research in wider fields. Fortunately, as mass production threatened to reduce every fresh idea to instant mediocrity, there flowered a new cult of individuality as it became more than ever imperative to sharpen one's own critical faculties by every available means—at the museum, at the theater, in books, art exhibits, and by close observation of nature to increase appreciation and understanding of design.

For example, a recent art exhibit in various media exploited the extraordinary revelation of form that occurs when white is placed against white, either in low relief or in varying tonalities. The eerie yet fascinating impression of this exhibit was recalled with the gift of some rare fossilized shells which had been buried from one million to fifteen million years in the sand of south Florida when Lake Okeechobee was a great inland sea and which were cast up where canals were being made a few years ago near the present lake.

For days these shells haunted their possessor with the strange beauty of their stark whiteness, subtle form and matte, unshell-like texture. Eventually they were made into a white-on-white centerpiece, mounted on squares of white-painted, grooved plywood and combined with some pale silvery yellow straw-flowers which seemed to share their eerie quality of timelessness (Plate 166). Thus any experience that brings a new awareness of design possibilities is of value and may furnish us with individual and exciting ideas making even a simple table decoration a creative adventure. Today's availability of such experiences gives us a new freedom of expression and increases our power of observation. Even the present interest in making "abstract" flower arrangements has value for those who really try to grasp the meaning of an abstraction, for they learn not only to assess plant material for its line, color, and form, but for its basic impact upon the imagination, free from old formulas and clichés.

There is no need to follow any specific style literally, even in period interpretations, unless required to be authentic at the flower show. As for styles for the home they are best chosen to stimulate personal expression in a spirit congenial to our own taste. In a modern house which emphasizes sophistication in its simplicity, as utilitarian a thing as a casserole may be endowed with great style and distinguished craftsmanship (Plate 168). Another house, equally sophisticated, may have an air of gleaming elegance, with lightness of color and form in table appointments. In this context, periods can be mixed at one and the same table if there is a fundamental compatibility in the styles selected, a definite, overall design purpose, and a firm decision as to the degree of formality or caprice which one wishes to achieve.

In the 1950's and '60's it was discovered that unadulterated modern could be rather obvious and lacking in warmth and personality. Some of the most interesting modern rooms today are apt to be enlivened with occasional objects from another century or with a collection of objects which reflect a special interest of the owners through the years. Small bronzes or art objects which look modern but are actually treasures from an ancient civilization add immense distinction as well as an element of drama and surprise (Plate 167). Such accessories are, of course, beyond the means of most people, but the same principle may be followed on a more modest budget. On a modern table with baroque overtones, even a bowl or compote from the comparatively recent but long-neglected period of Art Nouveau lends its own exuberant version of the unexpected. Or, delicate colors and gleaming textures borrowed from the 18th century might increase the air of elegance of a table setting with French porcelain of surrealist design, Steuben glass, and Jensen silver. Another person might use the same table appointments yet prefer to display them on a tablecloth of rough silk or a deep piled fabric and would choose a subdued, quiet color scheme taken from a cubist painting. So vast is the diversity of today's market that appropriate combinations for every temperament are available.

An intelligent evaluation of one's own preference and a regard for the special circumstances of an occasion can have a great deal to do with the success of setting a table for "company" today. We live in an age not only of individuality but also of casualness. Parties, more often then not, just happen on the spur of the moment. Informality is the usual order of the day, and any hostess, whether by nature a casual person or a perfectionist who really prefers formality, must be ready to cope at a moment's notice with all sorts of guests from a flock of grandchildren to her most fastidious and formal friends. Her reaction to this informal trend may be reflected in her individual solution to the problem.

An impromptu party may seem attractive and enjoyable by reason of its very spontaneity. But basically it requires planning of one sort or another to achieve this atmosphere. With imagination and quick thinking, the naturally casual person makes the most of whatever material presents itself. She depends on sturdy well-coordinated equipment with a few handsome props which may be added on special occasions. Her flower arrangements are usually made on the inspiration of the moment in much the same spirit as her casual way of gardening. If her chrysanthemums sprawl because she has not had time to tie them up, she will cut them and use their curving stems to advantage on the table, letting them tumble over the edge of an old brown basket in a gay spirit of country charm. Another day, when cutting back a straggling bed of applemint, she may find the clippings too beautiful to throw away and make a low fragrant wreath of them surrounding the swirled funnel of an earthenware pudding mold, accenting it with silver moon roses. This is a Gothic wreath if ever there was one, naïve in the French sense of the word *"naif,"* which is defined as natural, of an innocent freshness, without artifice (Plate 131). This spirit is at home on her simple porch with trestle table, and an old Southern colonial kitchen sideboard with pewter and colorful pottery although there is nothing Gothic there except the essential mood.

But the perfectionist whose house exemplifies traditional elegance must find another way of adapting informality, when necessary, to her formal background. In a dining room with 18th-century or federal detail, the lighter forms found in French provincial faïence or reproductions thereof would provide a gay, make-believe sort of rustic charm typical of the period which would suit her to a "T." A covered tureen in the shape of a fruit or vegetable flanked by little wicker baskets filled with violets or lilies of the valley could serve as centerpiece. Grandchildren, as a reward for careful handling of lovely things, would be entranced to have their soup in a bowl shaped like a lettuce leaf and might acquire new enthusiasm for scalloped fish if served in a "baby whale" ramekin of Canton blue earthenware. Even for a picnic the perfectionist will devote her special faculty for organization and orderly thinking to planning in advance for well-considered equipment so that a spur-of-the-moment outing will avoid the confusion which to her is anathema. The very same perfectionist who made the exquisite *cartonage* temple illustrated in Plate 77 is noted for the individual picnic baskets with which she provides her guests at alfresco concerts, weekly summer events at Castle Hill in Ipswich, Massachusetts. Painted a delicate mauve, the baskets hold fuchsia-colored napkins and pale green plastic cups and plates. Even the food, which is always of gourmet distinction, is planned to accord with the color scheme.

Quite different in temperament is an artist who entertains in a frankly Bohemian spirit. She has cupboards full of antique china and glass and also collects small pieces of modern sculpture (Plate 169), fascinating Orientalia, and an amazing assemblage of pottery and porcelain cats, both antique and modern. She likes to bring these treasures out, a few at a time, making imaginative combinations of them whether on the regular dining-room table or on a small table for two or three in the living room. The result is always visually unusual and exciting.

These are only a few of the possibilities for an approach to table decoration whether for everyday or for an important occasion. There are endless ways of creating an atmosphere of casual charm or one of elegance and distinction. How does one choose? The question to ask is not "what style shall I follow" but "what sort of a person am I." In this jet age, fashions change from one day to the next and one's own personality is the only fixed star.

Notes

INTRODUCTION

1. Ferrari, *Flora,* p. 437. These particular flowers were dried flowers recommended "to make a perpetual Spring at a banquet out of season," which seems to indicate that fresh flowers might have been used when available.

2. Marsden, *Palmyra of the North,* p. 199.

CHAPTER ONE

1. According to O.E.D. (1898), Walpole himself coined this word: "In Vertue's *Annecd. Painting,* 1786. IV 106 . . . 'The domestic called a Gardiner . . . will remain the Gardiner, the projector I should propose to denominate a Gardenist.' "

2. Le Grand d'Aussy, *Histoire de la Vie Privée des François,* Vol. 3, pp. 252–253.

3. Wright, *Account of . . . Castlemaine's Embassy,* p. 54.

4. *Ibid.,* p. 54.

5. Edgeworth, *Chosen Letters,* p. 276.

6. Bea Howe, *Decorating the Victorian Table,* "Country Life," Jan. 7, 1960, p. 10.

CHAPTER TWO

1. Gilliers, *Le Cannameliste Français,* p. 107.

2. Polo, *The Book of Ser Marco Polo,* Vol. 1, pp. 301–302.

3. Le Grand d'Aussy, *op. cit.,* Vol. 3, pp. 343–345.

4. Marsden, *op. cit.,* p. 238.

5. Medieval Catalogue No. 7, London Museum, 1940, p. 293. "Moulds for the stamping of sweet cakes were known in Gallo-Roman times. They reappear in the 15th and 16th centuries when they were very common in parts of Europe."

6. Wright, *op. cit.,* p. 55.

7. As quoted by W.B. Honey in *Dresden China,* pp. 22–23.

8. Le Grand d'Aussy, *op. cit.,* Vol. 3, pp. 300–301.

9. Mourey, *Le Livre des Fêtes Françaises,* p. 167. The original description of this fete is found in *Les Divertissemens de Versailles* by Félibien, p. 5.

10. Mourey, *op. cit.,* p. 162.

CHAPTER THREE

1. Athenaeus, *The Deipnosophists,* Vol. VII, p. 143.

2. Piozzi, *The Intimate Letters of Hester Piozzi . . . ,* p. 217. "But what fellows those old Romans were, after all! Fetching [as they actually did] Oysters from England and Roses from Egypt for one evening's entertainment. . . . " (Editor's note: Martial, Epigrams VI, 80 *Ad Caesarem de rosis hibernis.*)

3. Le Grand d'Aussy, *op. cit.,* Vol. 2, pp. 319–321 and Vol. 3, pp. 273–274.

4. Power, *The Goodman of Paris,* pp. 242, 244.

5. Victor Gay, *Glossaire Archéologique du Moyen Age et de la Renaissance,* Paris, 1887–1928, Vol. 1, under "Fleurs."

6. Cunningham (ed.), *Extracts from the Accounts of the Revels . . .* , p. 27.

CHAPTER FOUR

1. Le Grand d'Aussy, *op. cit.,* Vol. 3, pp. 273–274.

2. *Ibid.,* Vol. 3, p. 286.

3. Henri Havard, *Dictionnaire de l'Ameublement et de la Décoration,* Paris, 1887–90, Vol. 1, under "Fleurs."

4. McDougal, *Two Royal Domains of France,* p. 202.

5. Le Grand d'Aussy, *op. cit.,* Vol. 3, p. 399.

6. Denis Diderot, *Enclycopédie,* Paris, 1751–80, Vol. VI, p. 866.

7. The identity of Hannah Glasse has been a subject of some controversy. For a long time the writer of the many cookbooks under this name (or variations thereof) was thought to be Dr. John Hill, a literary adventurer. (See Cooper: *The English Table in History and Literature,* London, 1929.) However, a more recent book, Nancy Spain's *Mrs. Beeton and Her Husband,* London, 1948, in a footnote re Hannah Glasse on p. 18 proves that she was a woman, and carried on a long feud with a rival cookbook writer, Ann Cook.

8. Le Grand d'Aussy, *op. cit.* Vol. 3, pp. 288–289.

9. La Tour du Pin, *Journal . . .* , Vol. 2, p. 143.

10. *Ibid.,* Vol. 2, p. 242.

11. Napier, ed., *A Noble Boke off Cookry,* Intro., p. viii.

12. Beauvilliers, *The Art of French Cookery,* Intro., pp. xi and xii. (Recipes for cherries *en chemise* are found in Menon's *La Science du Maître d'Hotel,* Paris, 1768, p. 77 and in *The Cook and Housewife Manual* by Mrs. Margaret Dods, Edinburgh, 1828, p. 432.)

13. Ferrari, *op. cit.,* p. 396.

14. Mme. G., *Le Bouquet de Sentiment* ("Manière de Grouper les Fleurs," p. 106 and "Allegorie des Couleure," p. 110).

15. Félibien, *op. cit., Les Divertissemens de Versailles,* p. 6.

16. Marsden, *op. cit.,* p. 87.

17. Wharton, *Salons, Colonial and Republican,* p. 253.

18. Singleton, *The Story of the White House,* Vol. 1, p. 213, as quoted from Jessie Benton Fremont's *Souvenirs of My Time.*

19. Exhibition Catalogue, *Dinner with the Presidents,* The Art Institute of Chicago, *c.* 1961, p. 6.

CHAPTER FIVE

1. Le Grand d'Aussy, *op. cit.,* Vol. 3, p. 292 ff.

2. *Ibid.,* Vol. 3, p. 295.

3. Bernardi, *L'Art de Donner des Bals et Soirées,* p. 251 ff.

4. Jane Carlyle, *A New Selection of Her Letters,* pp. 188–189.

5. James Smith Colburn, "Personal Memoirs, 1801," unpublished ms., privately owned, p. 42.

CHAPTER SIX

1. Havard, *op. cit.,* under "Nef."

2. It is amusing to know that a piece of the "sword" of a swordfish satisfied all concerned, in the Middle Ages, as a "unicorn's horn," and that the swordfish is still sometimes referred to in France as *licorne de mer,* or unicorn of the sea. See *Nouveau Petit Larousse,* Paris, 1948, under "narval" and "licorne."

3. Le Grand d'Aussy, *op. cit.,* Vol. 3, pp. 247 and 258. King Charles V had "cups and goblets of crystal" (Vol. 3, p. 225) which may also have been treasured by Francis I. Crystal was greatly valued as it was thought to turn cloudy if the wine was poisoned. In Vol. 3, p. 186, Le Grand d'Aussy says that when the French gave crystal vessels to the Spaniards in exchange for gold the Spaniards were amazed that they would prefer gold to such rare beauty.

4. Havard, *op. cit.,* under "Milieu" (quoted from 1697 "Inventory of the Crown").

5. Le Grand d'Aussy, *op. cit.,* Vol. 3, p. 395.

6. Edgeworth, *op. cit.,* p. 126. (Madame Ouditot, an old lady of 72 who had known Rousseau in her youth told this anecdote to Maria Edgeworth in Paris in 1803.)

7. As quoted by Kathryn C. Buhler in Booklet on *Mount Vernon Silver,* Mt. Vernon Ladies Association of the Union, Mt. Vernon, Va., 1957, pp. 49–50 and 53–55.

8. Booklet, *Mount Vernon China,* Mt. Vernon Ladies Association of the Union (2nd edition, revised), Mt. Vernon, Va., 1962, p. 38.

CHAPTER SEVEN

1. Henri Clouzot, *Les Émailleurs Verriers en France,* La Revue de l'Art, v. 28, 1910, pp. 285–300.

2. As quoted by Jean Gorely in *Old Wedgwood,* 1943, p. 44. (Robert Roberts, in *The House Servant's Directory,* also mentions a dessert frame, p. 121.)

3. Le Grand d'Aussy, *op. cit.,* Vol. 3, p. 303.

4. Stone, *Chronicles of Fashion,* Vol. 1, p. 116. Also, Beauvilliers, *op. cit.* Int., p. xi, says: "The Romans used to have their live fish under the table in vases from which they were taken and cooked in sight of the guests. We have an example of fish meandering on the royal table; in fine vases they would make a beautiful ornament for the plateau."

5. La Marche, *Mémoires,* Vol. 3, p. 195.

6. Paul Perrot, Director of Corning Museum of Glass, "Verre de Neuers," *Antiques* magazine, Dec., 1956, p. 562. See also La Marche, *op. cit.* Vol. 2, p. 350. Footnote on this page says that Gossuin de Vieuglire, Master glassmaker, delivered for the duke's table, in 1453, for a banquet at the Chateau de Lille, *"des plateaux de verre et une fontaine de verre."*

7. Aulnoy, *La Cour et la Ville de Madrid,* pp. 475–476. See also Foulche-Delbosc, ed., *Mme. d'Aulnoy's Travels in Spain* (1690), London, 1930, Introd., in which it is proved that Mme. d'Aulnoy never actually went to Spain. She was a writer of fairy stories and her account of Spain was lifted from various authentic contemporary writings and embroidered with romantic episodes. Her mother did spend some time in Spain (in the pay of the French government as an informer) and doubtless passed along to her daughter small details such as fashions in table decoration.

8. Honey, *op. cit.,* p. 101.

CHAPTER EIGHT

1. Capt. Jacques-Yves Cousteau, "Fish Men Discover a 2,200 Year-Old Greek Ship," in *National Geographic Magazine,* Jan., 1954., p. 19.

At the March, 1954 meeting of the Wedgwood Club in Boston a *patera* of Campanian black ware salvaged on this expedition was loaned by Dr. Harold E. Edgerton, one of the scientists connected with the recovery of the "Lost Cargo." The story of the expedition was presented by Jean Gorely, secretary of the Wedgwood Club, and illustrated with slides of the salvaging operation.

2. Ashmole, . . . *Ceremonies of the . . . Order of the Garter,* p. 611.

3. Calderon de la Barca, *Life in Mexico,* Vol. 2, p. 167.

CHAPTER NINE

1. Forks are mentioned in the 11th century (a Greek princess, bride of the Doge of Venice in 1071, is said to have possessed one, but merely as a curiosity for which she was condemned as unduly "soft" and luxurious). Sometimes used for fruits or perhaps oysters, forks were not used for meats until the 16th century and then only by great personages. See *Bulletin des Musées d'Art et d'Histoire, Bruxelles,* Janv.-Avr., 1943, "L'Acquisition d'une Trusse de Table de 1597."

2. See Helen Sprackling, "Fruit Trenchers of the Sixteenth and Seventeenth Centuries," *Antiques* magazine, July, 1960, p. 48.

3. Dorival, *La Peinture Française,* p. 218.

Glossary

automate (English, "automaton")—a piece of mechanism having its motive power so concealed that it appears to move spontaneously.

biscuit porcelain—unglazed porcelain with a matte white finish to resemble marble.

bosquet—a little grove or wooded area.

cameo glass—an ancient Roman type of ornamental glassware in which figures or scenes are carved in a layer of translucent glass over glass of another color.

cannameliste—confectioner; derived from *cannamele,* the word by which the ancients described sugar cane *(canna)* which was similar in taste to honey *(mele).*

cantharus—a Greek goblet with high curved handles, usually on a base.

celadon—a pale, bluish greyish green. In ceramics (notably Chinese and Korean) a light green-glazed ware admired for its resemblance to jade.

chinoiserie—a European style in art and decoration reflecting Chinese qualities and motifs.

Corinthian bronze—an alloy of gold, silver, and copper produced at Corinth.

corne d'Amalthée—Horn of Plenty, derived from the horn of the goat, Amalthaea, and which nourished Jupiter.

crystal—from Greek word, *krystallos,* meaning "clear ice." The name was applied to clear transparent quartz from which beautiful table appointments and other objects have been made since the days of the Ancients. The term crystal is applied today to clear white glassware of fine quality.

free-form—non-geometric shapes.

futurism—a movement in art (in Italy, *c.* 1910) which purported to express the dynamic energy of modern life, free from tradition and outworn forms.

girondole—derived from the Latin, *girare,* meaning "to revolve around"; the term *girondole* was first given in France to a certain type of fireworks which had a circle of *fusées* in cone formation; by analogy it was given to a type of candelabrum having a circle of lights arranged in the same manner, and also to a three- or four-tiered dessert stand of the same shape.

hautbois—oboe.

intaglio—deep-cut carving (the opposite of cameo which is in relief).

millefleur—(literally, "thousand-flower") a tapestry with an all-over pattern of flowers and foliage.

279

mobile—a construction or sculpture frequently of wire and sheet-metal shapes with parts that can be set in motion by air currents.

orfèvrerie—ornamental objects made of gold or silver.

origami—the art or process of Japanese paper-folding to form dolls, animals, etc.

Palladian—formal, grandiose designs in the Roman style created by the Renaissance architect, Palladio. This style was imported into England by Inigo Jones in the 17th century and was closely followed by architects of the Georgian period.

parquetry—a patterned wood inlay used especially for floors.

parterre—(literally, "on the ground") an intricate garden design to be looked at from above.

plateau—(plural, plateaux) as a table appointment, a raised base of wood, metal, mirror glass, or other material for the display of fruits and sweetmeats at the dessert.

stupa—a Buddhist shrine with a tower of many tiers representing various aspects of Buddhist symbolism.

surrealism—a modern French movement in art and literature that purports to express subconscious mental activities through fantastic or incongruous imagery or unnatural juxtapositions and combinations.

tazza (plural, *tazze*)—of Arabian derivation *(tassah)* meaning an ornamental shallow bowl or vase, usually mounted on a foot. Though a very old word it was not used in English until 1828 when this type of container became very fashionable for fruit at dessert. Its meaning still had to be explained in Mrs. Beeton's book of household management in 1868.

treen—(Old English, literally, "of a tree") wooden ware.

verre-de-Nevers—generic term for the type of glass made outstandingly at Nevers, France, in the 17th and 18th centuries in the Italian technique of enameled glass known as "lamp work."

Bibliography

The following books may be of interest in clarifying the reasons for changes in fashion:

Allen, B. Sprangue: *Tides in English Taste,* New York, 1958.

Chapuis, Alfred and Edmond Droz: *Les Automates,* Neuchâtel, Switzerland, 1949.

Clifford, Derek: *A History of Garden Design,* London, 1962.

Elst, Joseph, Baron van der: *The Last Flowering of the Middle Ages,* Garden City, N. Y., 1946.

Fleming, John: *Robert Adam and His Circle,* Cambridge, Mass., 1962.

Pearson, Lu Emily: *Elizabethans at Home,* Stanford, California, 1957.

Schmutzler, Robert: *Art Nouveau,* London, 1964.

Wellman, Rita: *Victoria Royal,* London, 1939.

ADDITIONAL SOURCES

Ashmole, Elias: *The Institution, Laws and Ceremonies of the Most Noble Order of the Garter,* London, 1672.

Athenaeus: *The Deipnosophists* (English translation by Charles Burton Gulick, Ph. D.), Cambridge, Mass., 1941.

Aulnoy, Marie Catherine Jumelle de Berneville, Baronne de: *La Cour et la Ville de Madrid* (Mme. B. Carey, ed.), Paris, 1874.

Beauvilliers, Antoine B.: *The Art of French Cookery* (a translation of *L'Art du Cuisinier* by the same author, Paris, 1814), 3rd edition, London, 1827.

Beeton, Mrs. Isabella Mary, ed.: *Beeton's Book of Household Management,* London, 1861 and 1868.

Bernardi: *L'Art de Donner des Bals et Soirées, ou Le Glacier Royal,* Brussels, 1845.

Calderon de la Barca, Mme. Frances Erskine (Inglis): *Life in Mexico* (1839), Boston, 1843.

Carlyle, Jane Welsh: *Jane Welsh Carlyle: A New Selection of Her Letters* (arranged by Trudy Bliss), New York, 1950.

Colburn, James Smith: "Personal Memoirs," unpublished manuscript, privately owned, 1801.

Coryate, Thomas: *Coryat's Crudities* (reprinted verbatim from 1611, ed.), 3 vols., London, 1776.

Cunningham, Peter, ed.: *Extracts from the Accounts of the Revels at Court in the Reigns of Queen Elizabeth and King James I,* London, 1842.

Dorival, Bernard: *La Peinture Française,* Paris, 1946.

Edgeworth, Maria: *Maria Edgeworth* (1767–1849), *Chosen Letters* (F. V. Barry, ed.), London, 1931.

Félibien, André: *Les Divertissmens de Versailles,* Paris, 1676.

Ferrari, Giovanni Battista: *Flora, ouero Cultura di Fiori,* Rome, 1638.

G., Mme.: *Le Bouquet de Sentiment,* Chalon, 1816.

Gilliers (Chef d'Office to the King of Poland): *Le Cannameliste Français,* Nancy, 1751.

Glasse, H.: *The Compleat Confectioner,* Dublin, 1762 and 1805.

Gothein, Marie Luise: *A History of Garden Art* (Walter Wright, ed., translated from the German by Mrs. Archer-Hind, M. A.), 2 vols., London, 1928.

Honey, William Bowyer: *Dresden China,* London, 1934.

La Marche, Olivier de: *Mémoires* (15th century, Beaune et Arbaumont ed.), 4 vols., Paris, 1883.

La Tour Du Pin, Henriette Lucie (Dillon) Marquise de: *Journal d'Une Femme de Cinquante Ans* (1778–1815), 4th ed., 2 vols., Paris, 1913.

Le Grand d'Aussy, P. J. B.: *Histoire de la Vie Privée des François* (J. B. B. de Roquefort, ed., 1st ed. 1782), 3 vols., Paris, 1815.

Marsden, Christopher: *Palmyra of the North: The First Days of St. Petersburg,* London, 1943.

May, Robert: *The Accomplisht Cook* or *The Art and Mystery of Cookery,* London, 1685.

McDougal, D.: *Two Royal Domains of France* (Versailles and the Tuilleries), London, 1931.

Mourey, Gabriel: *Le Livre des Fêtes Françaises,* Paris, 1930.

Napier, Mrs. Alexander, ed.: *A Noble Boke off Cookry* (15th century, reprinted verbatim from a rare manuscript in the Holkham Collection), London, 1882.

Perkins, John: *Floral Designs for the Table,* London, 1877.

Perrault, Charles: *Les Plaisirs de l'Isle Enchantée,* Paris, 1674.

Piozzi, Hester: *The Intimate Letters of Hester Piozzi to Penelope Pennington* (1788–1821), (Oswald G. Knapp, ed.), London, 1914.

Polo, Marco: *The Book of Ser Marco Polo* (1254–1323, Col. Sir Henry Yule ed.), 3rd edition, revised by Henri Cordier, London, 1929.

Power, Eileen, ed.: *The Goodman of Paris* (*Le Ménagier de Paris, c.* 1393), first translated into English, London, 1928.

Reade, Brian: *Regency Antiques,* London 1953.

Roberts, Robert: *The House Servant's Directory,* Boston 1828.

Singleton, Esther: *The Story of the White House,* New York, 1907.

Stone, Mrs. Elizabeth: *Chronicles of Fashion,* 2nd ed., 2 vols., London, 1846.

Wharton, Anne Hollingsworth: *Salons, Colonial and Republican,* Philadelphia, 1900.

Wright, Michael (Chief Steward of His Excellency's house at Rome): *Account of His Excellence Roger, Earl of Castlemaine's Embassy* (first published in Rome in Italian, 1687), London, 1688.

Index

288   *Index*